The Violet Flame

Ignite the Sacred Fire Within
to Transform Your Shadows,
Awaken Your Power and
Step into Your True Purpose

VIOLET SKIES

HAY HOUSE

Carlsbad, California • New York City
London • Sydney • New Delhi

Published in the United Kingdom by:
Hay House UK Ltd, 1st Floor, Crawford Corner,
91–93 Baker Street, London W1U 6QQ
Tel: +44 (0)20 3927 7290; www.hayhouse.co.uk

Text © Violet Skies, 2026
Interior images © Shutterstock

The moral rights of the author have been asserted.

All rights reserved. No part of this book may be reproduced by any mechanical, photographic or electronic process, or in the form of a phonographic recording; nor may it be stored in a retrieval system, transmitted or otherwise be copied for public or private use, other than for 'fair use' as brief quotations embodied in articles and reviews, without prior written permission of the publisher.

The information given in this book should not be treated as a substitute for professional medical advice; always consult a medical practitioner. Any use of information in this book is at the reader's discretion and risk. Neither the author nor the publisher can be held responsible for any loss, claim or damage arising out of the use, or misuse, of the suggestions made, the failure to take medical advice or for any material on third-party websites.

A catalogue record for this book is available from the British Library.

Tradepaper ISBN: 978-1-83782-450-2
E-book ISBN: 978-1-83782-453-3
Audiobook ISBN: 978-1-83782-451-9

10 9 8 7 6 5 4 3 2 1

This product uses responsibly sourced papers, including recycled materials and materials from other controlled sources. For more information, see www.hayhouse.co.uk

The authorized representative in the EU for product safety and compliance is Penguin Random House Ireland, Morrison Chambers, 32 Nassau Street, Dublin D02 YH68, Ireland. https://eu-contact.penguin.ie

Printed and bound by CPI Group (UK) Ltd, Croydon CR0 4YY.

Praise for Violet Skies and The Violet Flame

'The world needs The Violet Flame – its time is now! Whether you've worked with The Violet Flame before or are just beginning your journey with this extraordinary frequency, this book is an incredibly wise and powerful guide to helping you really transform your life. It will take you on a healing and transformational journey with the Violet Flame that will shift how you experience the world forever. Everyone needs to activate and connect with Violet Flame!'
ESTELLE BINGAM, HOLISTIC THERAPIST, HEALER,
AND AUTHOR OF *Manifest Your True Essence*

'Violet has created the ultimate guide to the violet flame for experiencing transformation and spiritual liberation!'
KYLE GRAY, BEST-SELLING AUTHOR OF *Angels Are with You Now*

'Violet is the Violet Flame personified. This is her superpower and the world needs it right now.'
KAREN KAY, BEST-SELLING AUTHOR OF *Fairy Whispering*

'This book is pure alchemy. Violet has created something sacred – a guide that not only demystifies the Violet Flame but invites you into a deeply personal journey with it. As someone who works with energy and shadow every day, I found this book to be both powerful and practical. It's like being handed a torch of ancient wisdom, lit with love and purpose. If you're ready to meet your shadow with grace and awaken your magic, this is the book to hold close.'
EMMA GRIFFIN, AUTHOR OF *The Witch's Way Home*

For my 14-year-old self: your voice is now free.

And to my darling Nanna: through your eternal sleep, I awakened.

Contents

List of Practices and Rituals   ix

Introduction   xi

Chapter 1:   A Sacred Secret   1

Chapter 2:   Keepers of the Flame   23

Chapter 3:   Illuminating Shadows   41

Chapter 4:   Forgiveness Flame   63

Chapter 5:   Unified Flame   85

Chapter 6:   Glow Up   113

Chapter 7:   Igniting Higher Purpose   137

Chapter 8:   Lighting the Way   159

Chapter 9:   Returning to One   185

Final Thoughts   197

Acknowledgments   207

About the Author   209

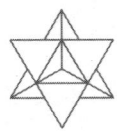

List of Practices and Rituals

Creating Your Own Violet Flame Altar	xxiv
Invoking the Flame	15
Becoming a Keeper of the Flame	33
Trusting Your Triggers to Teach	48
Choosing Change	59
Practicing Self-Forgiveness	71
Forgiving Others	81
Coming into Inner Union	96
Reconnecting with Your Inner Child	102
Uniting the Holy Trinity	107
Setting Intentions	122
Connecting with Intuition	133
Clearing Karmic Residues	143

Dancing with the Violet Flame	149
Activating the I AM Presence	155
Stepping Through the Infinity Gateway	169
Crafting a Daily Personal Prayer	177
Becoming Your Future Self	181
Birthing the New Earth with the Violet Flame of Unity	193
World Healing	200

Introduction

What if I told you that you could directly access a powerful force; one that has the ability to transform almost anything in your life?

A force that will burn through every aspect of your existence, transmuting any limitation and illuminating you from within.

A force so strong it can change the direction of humanity yet, mostly, it's been kept hidden for hundreds of years.

Within the pages of this book, I will share this secret with you…

✦

The Violet Flame is an etheric alchemical fire that courses through every atom of creation. A high-vibrational violet light, it spans timelines, dimensions, realms, and realities with the ability to transform energy. It's one of the most life-changing spiritual forces you can harness.

When you connect with the Violet Flame – and I will show you how – it will feel like a multitude of rebirths are simultaneously happening as you shift and reshape the meaning of life, and who you are within that. It can transform every illusion, belief, and program that stands in the way of you accessing love in its purest, most universal form.

The Violet Flame will:

- support you in transmuting guilt, resentment, and shame so you can forgive yourself and others

- remind you of your wholeness through inner union and assist in balancing your feminine and masculine energies

- clear karma on individual, ancestral, and collective scales

- bring freedom and liberation so you can express yourself fully and live passionately

In essence, the Violet Flame is a divine fire that burns away the surface layers and delves deep into the heart of your being, illuminating everything that prevents you from truly understanding and embodying love.

When we speak of love in relation to the Violet Flame, we don't mean the kind that's so often depicted in the movies, or broadcast via our TV screens. It's not the love we've been conditioned to think of in terms of romance, drama, or personal connection. The Violet Flame awakens us to something much deeper, much more profound. It calls us to experience the truth of love; one that's unconditional, all encompassing, universal.

In our purest form, we are made of this love. It's encoded in every cell of our being, and can be felt as a seed planted deep within the heart. The Violet Flame burns away the obstacles that separate us from this truth. It strips us of the layers of fear, conditioning, and shame, revealing the purity of our soul and our innate capacity to be pure universal love. This love is not personal; it transcends the ego and all dualities. It's not something we can possess or measure. This love exists beyond time and space and unites all things.

To live as universal love is to see with the heart's unclouded eyes. The desire or need to be loved by another dissolves, and you fall into holy surrender. As you realise you are already love, you become free. This brings about divine flow, and you truly open to the abundance of life. You become totally humbled by the concept of existence, no longer needing to grasp, to control, or to possess. You arrive at the realization that everything that's here, that you're experiencing, is here for you. You can allow and embrace all of life and in turn, all of yourself.

The Violet Flame opens you to the presence of God, Spirit, Source, the Creator, the universe, Divine Beloved (whichever term resonates for you), enabling you to be in presence with each moment, experiencing real, deep intimacy with life itself. You come into union entirely. This is the nature of the Flame, and through this fire you come into the fullness of what you're here to experience and be.

I'll be discussing the origins of the Violet Flame in more detail later. You may know of its strong association to Saint Germain – the ascended master who discovered it back when he walked the Earth. There are other keepers of the Violet Flame, too, all sharing its powers as a bridge to expanded consciousness, personal freedom, divine union, and universal love. As you begin to work with the meditations and exercises in this book, you'll also learn how to connect with these Keepers of the Flame, to help you on your journey to igniting the powers within you.

My Sparked Awakening

The first time I connected with the Violet Flame was during my early twenties. I was in a near-fatal car accident, having fallen asleep at the wheel of my car on the motorway. I woke to find I'd drifted across two lanes and was headed for the central reservation. To avoid colliding with oncoming traffic on the other side of the motorway, in that instant, I swerved. My car rolled across three lanes and hit two trees, which slowed the vehicle but by the time it stopped it was completely crushed in around me.

I was cut out of the car by the fire service and rushed to hospital in an ambulance. Everyone was in disbelief when I was discharged just three days later with nothing more than a few minor injuries. The emergency services claimed it was a miracle I was alive.

Once home from the hospital, sleep became a challenge. Every time I closed my eyes, I'd drift off only to be met by the same vivid recurring dream: I was back at the scene of the accident, hovering in mid-air, around 330ft (100m) above my car, looking down at my body inside the crushed vehicle. Two angelic beings of pure light would appear on either side of me, then a bright violet beam would surround us. At this point, the angels would gently link arms with me and assist me in floating back down to my physical body. Once they reconnected me to my body, I'd wake up suddenly. This dream repeated every time I fell asleep, over and over, until the doctors diagnosed it as PTSD. At the time, I was prescribed medication and eventually the dreams stopped.

With my awareness where it is now, I've come to realize it was Archangel Zadkiel and Lady Amethyst who, with the presence of the Violet Flame, were assisting me on that day. It wasn't part of the divine plan for my life to come to an end, and there was far more for me to do on this Earth plane.

Having a near-death experience certainly changed me in unexpected ways. After the accident, I was challenged with the concept that I'd 'escaped death.' Surely, there must be a reason I didn't die. What was I here to do?

Yet I carried on with my life, finding anything to distract me from going within. Part of me didn't want to know why I was still on Earth when I *should* have died; the responsibility of that felt too heavy.

I found myself using unhealthy coping mechanisms to deal with what I was processing from my near-death experience, as well as other past, painful challenges. I began pushing down and suppressing the shadows and often found myself plummeting into periods of deep depression or anxiety. I'd party hard, drink myself into oblivion, or take other substances, and there were several occasions when I ended up in very dangerous situations, from which I somehow managed to escape.

The turning point came when my dear Nanna passed in 2014. It's often through grief that we can access deeper levels of love, and the grief I felt after the death of my Nanna blasted my heart wide open. It was the catalyst for me moving through a period of expansive spiritual awakening.

In an instant, my awareness completely shifted and I was living in a completely different world. Everything I previously thought I knew was no longer my truth. The universe placed the right people on my path who supported, taught, and guided me through this period.

This is when I began to work with the Violet Flame in a more conscious, intentional way as I opened myself up to Spirit and the unseen realms. It was a process of deep soul remembering, transforming built-in programs to recall the universal truths forgotten over time. The most important ones: that we're infinite beings with unlimited potential, that everything is a vibrational frequency, life is made up of paradoxical cosmic jokes, we're all interconnected as one, and real magic is everywhere.

For the past decade, I've been on what many would call a healing journey, cultivated through developing a deeper awareness of the Self. My main intention was to open myself up so I could seek what was beyond the perceived limitations I'd always been accustomed to, so that I could be free in my expression.

I've experienced many realms, had many rebirths, and devoted myself to the path of liberation, expansion, growth, and inner union. Throughout this time, I've explored many different spiritual teachings, trained in many different healing modalities, cultivated a deep connection with myself through developing a multilayered understanding of Self, and have gained a whole toolbox of practices that have supported me in navigating life.

Introduction

My personal journey to get to this point hasn't been linear or easy. It's been messy, raw, and deeply humbling. However, every experience – the highs and the heartbreaks – has led me back to one truth: Every challenge we face is intended to show us the way home to universal love and union.

And one constant throughout it all has been the Violet Flame. It's been the most significant tool that has supported me. And the beauty of the Violet Flame? It's already right here for us. We carry it with us always, it can never get lost, can never be taken away, and we can connect with it any time we please.

My work is now rooted in creating safe spaces for others to explore their inner worlds, reclaim their true selves, step into their power, and express themselves unapologetically. My mission is to assist people in remembering their divinity and connect to the magic that's always been their birthright.

This book is an extension of that mission. It's my way of offering the wisdom I've gathered, the practices I've developed, and the lessons I've learned with the hope that it will illuminate your path as much as the Violet Flame has illuminated mine.

At my core, I deeply believe in the infinite potential of the human spirit. I've walked through my own shadows, felt the weight of my own doubts, and emerged with the understanding that every one of us is capable of profound transformation.

The Invitation

I want to revisit a moment in time with you, exactly four weeks before the deadline to submit my book proposal to Hay House.

I'd reached for my laptop over and over, and every time I'd gazed at my screen, I was met with resistance.

A paradox was playing out. I knew this book was here inside me – that it was already written, that my soul knew it was already done, and that life was guiding me here. Yet, every time I sat at the keyboard, willing myself to bring it through, the same thing happened: my neck muscles tightened, a lump formed in my throat as I swallowed, and all I could hear was the deafening scream of silence.

You see, I never really envisioned myself as an author. In fact, the written word has been one of the most persistent blocks I've experienced throughout my life. And yet, here I was, writing a book on the Violet Flame, the most powerful tool there is for transformation and alchemy. So naturally, it brought forward one of my own biggest shadows to heal in the process – feeling safe enough to write things down.

As a child, I'd loved writing stories and poetry. English, along with art, were my favorite subjects at school. As a teen, I'd write down my feelings to process my emotions around what I was experiencing: it was therapeutic for me. However, at around 14 years old, I stopped journaling due to an incident where my privacy was violated and my inner world exposed. Writing this book has been one of the most significant challenges in my life to date, especially as my connection to the Violet Flame has always been something I've kept private – until now.

With this in mind, am I feeling vulnerable speaking on this? Yes.

Am I scared to birth this into the world for people to read? Yes.

Would it feel way more comfortable right now to stop writing this book? Yes.

If I stopped writing this book, would it be serving my highest good and the highest good of all? No!

The Violet Flame is to be shared.

So here I am, practicing what I preach: liberating myself through authentic expression, shining a light on the shadow aspects that want to keep me small, trusting the trigger to teach, feeling the fear and doing it anyway. And you'll learn to do the same as you journey through this book.

Another paradox is also playing out here: This book is not even about me, it's about you.

It is for you, and yet it is for me, too. It is for my teenage self who stopped writing because she built a protective wall around her so high that over time her words got lost.

I've shared this as I want to let you know: I'll also be embarking on a healing journey with you as I write the pages you're now reading. Seek comfort in knowing that we're moving through this together.

I'm writing this book as I believe we're all being called to rise into our highest potential. The challenges we face – personally and collectively – are not here to defeat us. They're here to awaken us: for on the other side of every challenge is a gift. The

Violet Flame offers us a way through, a way to heal, to grow, and to remember the truth of who we are.

This book is my offering to you – a heartfelt guide to working with the Violet Flame so you can embrace the fullness of your being. The Violet Flame meets you exactly where you are, ready to support you as you are. You don't need to be perfect. You don't need to have it all figured out.

You don't need to be anyone other than who you are, right in this moment, to begin this journey. The Violet Flame is within you, waiting to be activated. My role is simply to be a guide, to hold up a mirror so you can see the beauty and light that's always been you.

So, I ask you this: Are you ready for blazing transformation, to illuminate the truth of your heart, and shine a light on who you came here to be?

Not only a 'Yeah… well, I know something in my life needs to change, and I think it's time to welcome something new.'

I mean, are you *really* ready? The type of ready that comes from a full-body *'YES, I have goose bumps, and I'm ready to set my soul on fire, transforming my life from the inside out.'*

This is an invitation to venture into the inner knowing that there's more to life than the eye can see, more to our human selves than we've currently explored, and more to this world than we've been taught.

It's an invitation to navigate shadows, seek clarity, experience expansion, and nurture a deeper connection with the Divine. This invitation is for you, as I know you wouldn't be here unless some part of you was ready to step into the magic of what's possible.

On that note, welcome, courageous soul.

Let's read on...

About This Book

Once you invoke the Violet Flame into your life, nothing will remain the same. It will shift everything in ways you cannot yet imagine. It will unlock new strands of DNA within you and open new pathways for your life.

This book is not only about the Violet Flame – it's about *you*. It's about reclaiming your true power, rediscovering your connection to the Divine, aligning with your soul's purpose, and coming into deeper union with the whole. Throughout these pages, you'll learn to move beyond the limitations of your past and rise into a new way of being – one that's more authentic, loving, and freeing.

When you embark on a spiritual journey, going through a period of awakening, feeling expansion, or tending to inner healing, it can be a transformative and enriching experience. However, it's important to note that we can often find ourselves entangled in a web of complexity. The sheer amount of information out there, the many diverse approaches to healing, and the range of spiritual modalities available can cause us to overcomplicate the path of awakening.

This can then steer us toward temporary solutions or superficial healing, leading us inadvertently into spiritual bypassing – where we avoid the necessary inner work and instead, we subconsciously use the external search for wholeness as another distraction. We jump from one thing to the next, like a kid in a candy store, without integrating anything fully. Meaning we completely dodge having to confront those deep-seated shadows that fuel our self-limiting beliefs and drive our unhelpful behavioral patterns.

Here, you can end up creating a reality for yourself that consists of repeated lessons, patterns, and loops. Though they may come packaged slightly differently each time, staying in these perpetual loops leaves little space for growth, expansion, or fresh new experiences.

You may also hear a lot of talk that only 'love and light' should be focused upon and be familiar with the concept of 'positive vibes only.' However, toxic positivity doesn't hold up for very long. While it's true that at our core we are manifestations of love, genuine illumination comes through facing and embracing our shadows. To truly access the universal love and light available to us, we must first confront and understand the areas within us that are devoid of love or that form decisions from fear-based beliefs and a lack mentality.

When we find the parts of ourselves that require acknowledgment, acceptance, and unconditional love, we can begin to transform the way we navigate life, helping us to respond to people, places, and situations differently. The world becomes our mirror. Seeing our own previous patterns playing out via others, through their reflection we gain deeper understanding of why people behave the way they do. Within this awareness comes a softening and we begin to view all life through the lens of compassion.

The key intention of this book is expansion through simplicity.

Using the simplicity of the Violet Flame.

It's important to remember: This book is an invitation, not a prescription. This book is also not a replacement for therapy. I share my own journey with you, offering what's worked for me, and you're encouraged to take what resonates and leave what doesn't. You may encounter resistance at times, and I invite you to sit with it. In my experience, resistance often holds the key to tremendous growth, healing, and freedom.

And here's the greatest secret I can share with you: You are already whole. Everything you seek is already within you. Wholeness is simply a matter of seeing beyond the illusion of lack – because anything rooted from lack is just fear (*more on this in Chapter 3, page 41*).

We are living in extraordinary times, a moment in history when humanity is being called to awaken to the truth of who we are, to remember the infinite potential we carry within us, and clear the threads that have kept us tethered to old paradigms of fear, separation, and limitation. It's a call for transformation, both personal and collective.

This book is for anyone who feels that call deep in their soul, a yearning to rise above the illusions of the world and connect with a deeper truth. Whether you're navigating a spiritual awakening, seeking healing from past experiences, or simply longing to live a more aligned and authentic life, the Violet Flame offers a way forward.

Why is this book important now? Because the world needs your light. As you grow, transform, and awaken, you don't just change your own life – you become an inspiration to others. Your healing ripples out into your relationships, your community, and ultimately the collective consciousness of humanity. This is the power of the Violet Flame: it transforms individuals, and it's also the very fabric of our shared reality.

So, as we now journey through these pages together, know that you are held by the Violet Flame. Its light surrounds you, its power flows through you. And embodying universal love and coming into union is inevitable.

Creating Your Own Violet Flame Altar

Before you enter the chapters, if you feel called to do so, you can create a Violet Flame altar so you have a devotional space to visit and return to as you read this book and complete the accompanying practices.

An altar is a place charged with intention and meaning. It becomes a powerful tool for centering energy, inviting transformation, and supporting your journey through reflection, rituals, meditation, and invocations.

Here are some suggestions of items you can include on your altar:

- **A candle:** A violet or purple candle to represent the Violet Flame. You can light this before you begin a practice as it's a beautiful way to open to prayer, meditation, or ritual.

- **Crystals:** Powerful amplifiers of energy, they can enhance your connection to the Violet Flame. Amethyst is strongly linked to the Flame as its vibration can bring feelings of peace and purification. Sugilite is another powerful crystal to work with as it holds the energy of transformation, as does charoite crystal.

- **Incense or essential oils:** Scents like lavender, frankincense, or sandalwood elevate the energy of a space. Oils can also be used to anoint the body on the third eye, heart, or feet. This serves as an act of self-care and brings feelings of presence and grounding. (*Please note: Always use a carrier oil when applying directly onto skin.*)

- **Symbols and imagery:** Images of angels or ascended masters, such as Saint Germain, can support you in connecting to the Violet Flame. You may also like to take some time to paint or draw the Flame on a small canvas and place it on your altar so it's amplified by your own creative energy. (*I will share more about the Keepers of the Flame in Chapter 2, page 23.*)

- **Personal items:** Anything that holds deep spiritual meaning for you can be included. This could be a piece of jewelry, a small journal for writing down intentions, or an object that symbolizes something you're working to release or transform. These items will help you personalize the altar and connect more deeply with the energies you're cultivating.

- **Plants and flowers:** Adding fresh flowers or a small plant brings the energy of life. Violets, lavender, or lilacs represent vitality and growth, echoing the essence of the Violet Flame.

Building an altar is a mindful, intuitive practice. Each item carries meaning, and its placement becomes an expression of your intentions:

1. Choose a location that feels inviting, peaceful, and energetically clear. It could be a corner, shelf, or even a portable tray or small box if you're limited on space.

2. Cleanse your chosen space. You can use herbs, incense, or sound (such as a drum, singing bowl, or your voice).

3. Place your chosen objects thoughtfully, allowing intuition to guide you. You might consider the spiritual associations of directions: East for air and new beginnings, South for fire and transformation, West for water and healing, North for earth and grounding. Most importantly, follow what feels right. Keep the space uncluttered and meaningful; it's a living altar that evolves with your journey.

4. Visit it regularly, changing items as your intentions shift, and let it serve as a reminder of the Violet Flame's transformative power.

CHAPTER 1

A Sacred Secret

'Remember who you are,'
the Violet Flame whispered through its flickers.
'You have been deep in amnesia for far too long.'

Into the fire, I replied: 'I don't even know
what is real anymore. In my mind, my heart.
Both seem in continuous battle with one another.
My vision is blurred by a haze of deep longing.
There is an ache within me that I can't seem to locate.
I yearn to live in a world that I don't feel exists.'

The Violet Flame gently answered through its illumination…
'Your yearning is for love, for freedom, for the
sweet surrender that comes from choosing union.
Your longing is to feel the presence of the Divine
Beloved, filling you with every breath you take.
You ache for the moment you finally find home, where
you are at peace. And yet, all of this already exists.
It is here for you now, as it lives within you.
You lack nothing. You are the bridge for Heaven on Earth.
And I am here to light the way.'

Within a heartbeat I knew, I was about to awaken to life,
in ways I hadn't experienced before.

The Violet Flame is a phenomenon that transcends the boundaries of language. It's not something that can be neatly defined, analyzed, or rationalized by our human minds. It exists in the realm of the experiential, where the heart understands what words cannot express. Like the mysteries of the universe, it operates on a frequency that we feel in our very being, even if we can't always comprehend it intellectually.

In our modern world, we're often taught to seek proof, to demand explanations, and to rely on logic or science to validate our experiences. Yet the most profound truths – the ones that shape us, heal us, and awaken us – rarely come packaged in the form of neat answers. They are felt. They are known, in a deep, quiet way that resonates with the core of who we are. This is the Violet Flame.

When you connect with the Violet Flame, you're not engaging with something external to you; you're awakening a part of yourself that's always existed. A part of you that connects you to the whole of creation. To truly understand the Violet Flame, you must step beyond the mind's need for explanation and into the heart's capacity to surrender to the mystery, so you can move through the unknown.

Consider the way you experience love, beauty, or a breathtaking sunset. You don't dissect these moments to understand them; you simply feel them, allowing them to move you, to transform you. The Violet Flame works in much the same way. Its essence is something to be lived. It's an invitation to open yourself to transformation and to trust that it will bring you exactly what you need in each moment.

As you embark on this journey with the Violet Flame, I encourage you to let go of any need to control or fully understand the experience. Instead, let yourself feel it. Notice the subtle shifts in your energy, the moments of clarity that arise, the gentle changes that begin to appear in daily life, and the new levels of wisdom and awareness you begin to connect to. Trust that its presence is real and that it will work in harmony with your highest good.

Some mysteries aren't meant to be logically solved; they're meant to take you on an adventure so you can make discoveries through experience. The Violet Flame is one such mystery, and it holds the power to awaken a part of you that's been waiting for this very moment.

I am glad you are still here, courageous soul.

The Powers of the Flame

As you connect with the Violet Flame – starting with the practice at the end of this chapter – you'll encounter its transformative energy in different forms. Let's explore what the Violet Flame symbolizes and the main areas in which it can become a guiding force for you in your life. In each chapter that follows, I'll go deeper into these areas and show you how, through connecting to the Violet Flame, you'll be able to nurture and liberate yourself.

Transformation: The Alchemy of Shadow Work

The Violet Flame represents transformation at its core. It allows you to face the shadows within yourself: those triggers and limiting beliefs that can hold you back or throw up heavy emotional reactions to what's being experienced. By working with the Violet Flame, you can embrace shadow work with grace, illuminating the parts of yourself you've been avoiding. This Flame helps you look at your shadows with a fresh perspective. They're not something to be ashamed of or to be pushed down, they're an invitation for growth. The Flame empowers you to integrate and transform these energies into opportunities for self-liberation; within these shadows lies a gift. It shows you that transformation is about learning from the past so you can evolve your choices to align with experiences that are more expansive and supportive.

Freedom: Liberation from Limitations

At the heart of the Violet Flame is the gift of freedom. It offers liberation from the constraints of the egoic mind – those patterns of fear, doubt, and limitation that keep you repeating old stories. It ignites within you hope, the type of hope that brings about change, as it reveals to you the illusions you've been living under – false beliefs about yourself, others, and the world. It dissolves the need to control and instead, its illumination invites you to live in flow. This freedom is the inner liberation of the soul. It's the type of freedom that can never be taken away, as it's who you've become at the core.

Forgiveness: Releasing Guilt and Resentment

Forgiveness is one of the Violet Flame's greatest gifts. It holds the energy of compassion, inviting you to forgive yourself and others with love and understanding. This sacred energy reminds you that forgiveness doesn't condone harmful actions, and it's important to acknowledge your experiences and how they made you feel. However, through forgiveness you liberate yourself. Forgiveness frees you from holding onto the past through coming into acceptance with what's been experienced and looking at life through the eyes of compassion. By forgiving, you reclaim your power and allow yourself to step fully into the present moment.

Divine Union: Balancing Masculine and Feminine Energies

The Violet Flame symbolizes the sacred dance between the masculine and feminine energies within you. It guides you to a state of divine union – where the action-oriented structure of the divine masculine meets the intuitive, nurturing flow of the divine feminine. In this wholeness, you move beyond duality and find harmony within. As you integrate these energies, you awaken to your authentic Self and embody the completeness that's always existed within you. The Violet Flame invites you to flow with the dance of creation, finding balance within the polarity.

Truth: Living in Alignment

To invoke the Violet Flame is to align with your truth. It inspires you to set clear intentions and live with integrity, authenticity, and purpose. It burns away illusions, revealing the core of who you are and what truly matters. When you orient your life with truth, you create space for deeper connection, greater fulfillment, and the clarity to walk a path of alignment with your soul's calling. In doing so, you can express yourself and create in a way that feels fulfilling and lights up your heart, in turn lighting up the hearts of others you encounter.

Purification: Establishing Boundaries and Enhancing Intuition

Purification is a key aspect of the Violet Flame. It helps you cleanse your energy field, transmuting any auric debris so you can maintain a clear, strong vibration. Purification also assists you in creating and then standing firm in your boundaries. The Flame sharpens your intuition and, with its presence, you can improve your ability to discern what aligns with your highest good, feeling safe in your interactions with the world rather than confused or drained. By working with the Violet Flame in this way, you step into energetic sovereignty: you find safety within yourself through transforming doubt, releasing control, developing a discernment, and navigating life from a place of clarity and confidence.

I AM Presence: Embodying Your Divine Essence

At its heart, the Violet Flame is a direct link to the I AM presence, which is the divine spark within each of us that connects us to creation (*more on this in Chapter 7*). It reminds you of your infinite nature and your role as cocreator of your reality. By connecting with the Violet Flame, you awaken to the understanding that you're not separate from the Divine/God/Source, you're a living expression of it. This awareness invites you to embody your divinity and live with purpose and intention as expressions of universal love and grace.

Karmic Clearing: Breaking Out from the Cycles of the Past

The Violet Flame will also burn bright to assist with clearing karma. It helps you resolve personal karma – patterns and lessons carried over from this and past lifetimes – as well as ancestral and collective karma that you may carry unconsciously. By working with the Flame, you can rewrite these energetic imprints, moving out from repeating cycles and choosing differently. In doing so, you free not only yourself but also those who come after you, as through changing your karma you're creating a new timeline.

Peace: Through Experiencing Oneness

The ultimate gift of the Violet Flame is peace. As you shed the layers of fear, illusion, and separation, you come to experience oneness with all of creation and move into a unity consciousness. This peace is a profound inner stillness and harmony that comes from knowing your connection to the Divine and all of what is. The Violet Flame shows you that you're never truly alone, as even the word alone contains all one. In this state of peace, you can be a source of calm and compassion for others, contributing to the collective awakening of humanity.

Shining a Light

Now let us look at the history of the Violet Flame, a frequency that holds the power to change our lives from the inside out. For centuries, spiritual seekers turned to this etheric flame for healing, to ignite awakening, and to bring about the alchemical process of internal and external transformation. Interestingly, you'll find some of its concepts also shared by theories of modern science, which may help you to understand it further.

In quantum physics, within the phenomenon of 'quantum entanglement' – where particles become connected and remain so, regardless of physical distance – we're taught about the interconnectedness of all things that transcend spatial constraints. The Violet Flame mirrors this scientific concept as it is universal, infinite, and has a boundary-defying essence.

Psychologist Carl Jung spoke of the collective unconscious – a shared part of our minds where universal symbols and experiences reside. Again, the Violet Flame, with its universal symbolism of transformation, resonates with this idea. It's a concept that speaks to everyone and can work with anyone who chooses to call upon it, across any physical time and space.

Whispers of the Violet Flame's existence have traveled far and wide over time, from the corridors of ancient civilizations, where mystics and sages once perceived it as a powerful force. This ethereal flame, with its radiant violet light beams, has continued to be intertwined through a multitude of cultures since.

Its presence can be found woven through the chronicles of humanity, and its flame will continue to burn infinitely through all of time and space, being a frequency that transcends temporal confines. It is part of the tapestry of creation; it is Spirit and therefore omnipresent.

The Violet Flame is deeply connected to the legend of Atlantis. It's said that it was gifted to the priests and priestesses of Atlantis directly from the Divine. A Temple of the Violet Flame was constructed as its physical home, one where people could receive its healing. The Atlanteans believed the Violet Flame had the ability to transmute all density from the physical, mental, emotional, and spiritual body of every individual. Its priests and priestesses used it to ensure all animals, people, and the Earth were kept harmonious and pure – it prevented imbalance and stopped dis-ease across the globe. However, as Atlantis fell, so did all knowledge of the Violet Flame.

In Ancient Egypt, the Violet Flame was embraced as a symbol of purification and spiritual ascension. Within the sacred rites of the Egyptian culture, the vibrant energy of the Flame was invoked to cleanse the soul, illuminating the path toward enlightenment. It was revered as a catalyst for inner alchemy.

Meanwhile, in the spiritual traditions of the East, the Violet Flame resonates with the concept of Kundalini, which is the life-force energy often referred to as a coiled serpent resting at the base of the spine. The activation of this life force is much like igniting the Violet Flame within. They both initiate a process of inner purification and awakening. This Eastern perspective views the Violet Flame as an essence capable of awakening dormant potentials and guiding individuals toward higher states of consciousness.

In today's Western societies, there seems to be very little written or published about the Violet Flame, yet more and more of us are beginning to feel drawn to its energy. The Violet Flame will have a vital part to play in this great awakening that we're currently experiencing here on Earth. Why has it been shrouded in secrecy, and why do we still see so little information about it today?

While many sacred teachings, powerful symbols, and transformative energies have been lost over time, especially with a collective shift toward more science-backed theories, the Violet Flame represents a force so potent, so transformative, that it shakes the very foundations of our consciousness. Those in positions of power – whether religious, political, or societal – have understood that humanity is easier to control when kept in a state of fear, confusion, and separation from our true divine nature.

The Violet Flame, with its ability to awaken us to our highest truth, liberate us from fear and separation, reminds us that we are sovereign, and shows us our innate power to create and transform our realities.

Burning Bright

As I've sat meditating with the Violet Flame, I've connected deeply with its messages on humanity. Humanity is at a pivotal moment in time where two potential timelines are possible: the Grand Rising, where we collectively return to love and create a New Earth, or the Great Reset, where we collectively choose fear, and the path of compliance continues.

The Grand Rising and the Great Reset

The Grand Rising is humanity's collective awakening – a conscious movement toward universal love, unity, and a cocreation of a New Earth that's founded on frequencies of compassion, authenticity, and interconnectedness. It's rooted in the concept of oneness, where we see ourselves in one another, embodying the understanding that what we do to others, we ultimately do to ourselves. Here, all life on Earth thrives together. In stark contrast, the Great Reset represents a timeline in which humanity succumbs to fear, relinquishing autonomy in exchange for perceived safety and stability. It's where we choose separation, which comes from feeding the concept that there's an external 'savior.' It's a path of compliance, where outside forces dictate the rules of existence, limiting our potential, and implementing nuanced cycles of control.

There are forces on this planet attempting to steer the collective consciousness toward choosing the Great Reset, as a few gain to profit from control of the masses. Due to this, much has been hidden from us, including ancient knowledge, teachings, practices, and wisdom. However, the systematic constructs upon which the world has been built are coming to an end, and the Grand Rising is inevitable.

The preparation we do now will depend on how easeful we find this transition. Currently, it may feel as though the world is shifting in ways that are uncomfortable to bear witness to. We must trust the process of this crumbling. As, often, when it feels like everything is falling apart, it actually means everything is coming together.

One thing's for sure: We're hearing the whispers of Spirit calling our souls home, to the truth of who we are, and we are remembering. Sensing the untapped potential within us, we're questioning and following our hearts to the places we feel more fulfillment, looking to retrieve the innate magic that we know already exists.

Harnessing the Violet Flame is no longer a practice confined to the forgotten pages of history; it's an empowering tool accessible to all. It's coming forward now during this great period of mass awakening to support the timeline of the Grand Rising. When we call in the Violet Flame, it opens up a new understanding of what we truly are, where we've come from, and our purpose on this planet. We are in a time of great transmutation and the reunion of that which has been split. There will be a desire to seek truth, to live free, and to dissipate the illusions that have been placed upon us. Many are already experiencing this.

As we move through this ascension process, deep shifts are happening. We're becoming more aware of our own shadows and raising awareness, changing our own responses to challenging experiences, and clearing karma. As humanity wakes from its slumber, intuition is developing, and more of us are activating our capacity for healing. Having the ability to tune in to frequencies that the human eye can't see is becoming the new normal.

The New Earth will see us living from our heart space. Some perceive that when we 'ascend' it means going somewhere else or leaving the planet altogether to live within a higher plane of existence. However, what ascension really means is that we get to experience Heaven here on Earth. We get to experience Utopia, while still being a human in the physical world.

Here, we'll move from logic to intuition. There will be peace, harmony, and unity. We'll experience oneness as our natural state of being. We'll be able to see energy, and it will be how we access knowledge and wisdom. We'll see all of the higher-dimensional realms. The illusion of separation will completely lift. We'll be multidimensional beings still living in this physical world with direct access to the unseen realms at the same time.

The Violet Flame is here to assist with this as it burns through all threads of density, clearing them so we can evolve together. This will bring cosmic justice, restoring balance as we move into this New Earth where we can forge a new essence of purity and unconditional love.

So, let's begin with the following practice, which aims to align your energy with the essence of the Violet Flame.

A Note to the Reader

Listening to guided meditations can help you fully immerse yourself in the visualizations. Audio recordings of the exercises and meditations throughout this book can be found in the audiobook version – available wherever you listen to audiobooks. Alternatively, you can try recording yourself reading it aloud and then play it back whenever you're ready.

Invoking the Flame

The first step to working with the Violet Flame is becoming aware of it within your own energy field. By welcoming the Violet Flame on a regular basis, hidden truths will begin to emerge, and synchronicities will start appearing. It will slowly invite you to embrace the process of metamorphosis and become increasingly aware of your own creativity.

There's nothing to fear when working with the Violet Flame; it is light and works for the highest good of all. It cannot burn you. Its energy always results in bringing deeper levels of love into our lives. However, change and transformation can feel uneasy – to step forward with true change, we must surrender to the unknown.

This is when working with the Violet Flame can feel uncomfortable, when we attempt to cling to control so we can stay in the perceived known. Action follows the mind, and often your ego mind will search for the known as it gives the illusion of it being safer there. You end up doing what you've always done, keeping yourself small because it's easier, while simultaneously feeling there's more within you to be expressed, explored, and experienced.

By calling upon the Violet Flame, you'll naturally begin to allow space for the unknown: the void, the place of possibility, where all is created and birthed from. This is where transformation lives and where your liberation lies.

Preparation for Invoking the Flame

1. Choose a quiet, comfortable place where you won't be disturbed. It can be anywhere that allows you to feel at peace – in your home, in nature, at your Violet Flame altar (see page xxiv), or even a designated meditation corner. The key is to ensure it is somewhere you can fully immerse yourself in the practice.

2. To elevate the energy of the space, you may want to burn incense, such as sandalwood or frankincense. Additionally, you can anoint yourself with lavender essential oil, known for its calming properties, which will assist in bringing you into presence and preparing your mind and body for meditation. Place some oil on your third eye (in the center of your forehead just above your eyebrows), on your heart, and on the base of your feet.

3. You can also hold any crystals that represent the Violet Flame for you – amethyst, charoite or sugilite are known to harmonize with the Violet Flame's energy.

4. Set a candle nearby, which you will light later in the practice. The flame of the candle will serve as a symbolic representation of the Violet Flame and its transformative power. This small but intentional act can help you focus your energy on your practice.

5. Before beginning any spiritual practice, it's important to set a clear intention. This acts as a guiding force that aligns your inner energy with what you want to move toward. In this case, your focus should be on connecting with the power of the Violet Flame. As you prepare yourself for this experience, quietly state your intention:

    'I open myself to the Violet Flame and welcome its presence into my life for my highest good and the highest good of all.'

You can tailor your intention to suit your needs – whether it's for healing, spiritual growth, cleansing, or transformation. Be mindful and deliberate with your intention, as this will help ground your energy and ensure you're fully present during the practice.

6. You can choose to sit or stand, but ensure that your spine is straight, promoting the free flow of energy through the body. Take a few deep breaths, inhaling deeply through the nose, feeling the lungs expand with each breath, and exhaling slowly through the mouth, releasing any tension from the muscles. With each breath, feel yourself becoming more grounded and centered in your body.

7. Now imagine roots growing from the base of your spine, down deep into the earth. These roots act as an anchor, connecting you to the earth's energy, providing stability and grounding. Feel the solidity of the earth beneath you and allow yourself to surrender as it holds the weight of your body. This grounding process will help you remain embodied throughout the practice.

Practicing Energetic Protection

There's a lot of information out there on practicing 'energetic protection' before embarking on any kind of spiritual work. Some of the simplest things you can do to assist with this are:

- **Visualization:** Imagine yourself surrounded by a protective source of light. I'd suggest a violet light as the Violet Flame transmutes all.

- **Crystals:** Hold a crystal that has strong protective properties, such as black tourmaline or shungite.

+ **Sound:** Say a simple affirmation aloud, such as, 'I AM Safe, Protected, and Loved.'

However, when you begin to connect consciously with the Violet Flame and you feel its presence, you realize that nothing other than pure universal love can penetrate your energy. You continuously feel the Violet Flame within you, so feeling the need to intentionally place energetic protection may become redundant as it's always there.

A really important point: the concept of energetic protection is not to be confused with discernment. Discernment is always something we need to tune in to, as it's part of our intuition and it shapes our inner compass.

Connecting to the Violet Flame

You're now ready to enter into the visualization process; a powerful tool that will allow you to create a visual and energetic connection to the Violet Flame.

1. Start by closing your eyes and imagining yourself in a serene space where you feel calm and open to the vastness of the universe. It could be a tranquil natural setting, such as a meadow, or forest, or beside a body of water, or it could simply be a vast expanse of light. Trust your intuition to guide you to a place that feels right.

2. At the center of your heart space, visualize a violet fire flickering gently. This is no ordinary flame – it is the Violet Flame, radiating with cosmic energy and vibrant, transformative power. The violet light shimmers and dances, inviting you to connect with its energy. Notice how the Flame feels. Is it warm, cool, or somewhere in between? Take in the sensations that arise as you focus your

attention on it. Feel its energy, and sense that it holds the ability to cleanse, heal, and alchemize all denser energies into light.

3. Now, as you take a deep breath, imagine drawing this violet light through your body with each inhale. Feel the energy of the Violet Flame illuminating every cell within you. As it flows through your body, the light spreads, expanding through your entire being. It fills your head, neck, shoulders, arms, chest, and down into your abdomen, legs, and feet. With every inhale, the light grows stronger, and with every exhale, you feel yourself soften and surrender.

4. As you continue to breathe deeply, feel yourself becoming one with the Violet Flame. Allow its flames to dance around and within you, completely encompassing you in its radiant light. You are now fully connected to the transformative energy of the Violet Flame.

5. Anchor the Violet Flame through a heartfelt invocation – this can help you establish a deeper connection with its energy, serving as a bridge between you and the Flame, calling its presence into your experience. Speaking your invocation aloud adds power, as your voice carries your unique vibration and will amplify your intention. You can either use the one I suggest here or you can mindfully create your own. This can be a prayer, affirmation, or simply asking to connect with the Violet Flame.

> 'I call the Violet Flame to me,
> as in its essence I AM free.
> I AM open, I AM aware.
> Violet Flame, I feel you here.
> I AM one with this cosmic surge,
> the Violet Flame and I now merge.

> *I AM harmony, I AM in sync,*
> *with the Violet Flame I truly link.*
> *I AM the embodiment of divine light,*
> *I AM the Violet Flame burning bright.'*

Feel the power of your words as you recite them. Each line reinforces your connection with the Flame, affirming your openness to its transformative energy. This is your moment to embrace it fully, knowing that its energy will assist in purifying and uplifting you.

6. Now that you've invoked the Violet Flame, visualize it merging completely with your being. The Flame is within you – intertwining with your own energy field, transforming any density so you start to become lighter.

7. As you breathe, notice how your body feels. There may be a sensation of lightness, as the Flame works to dissolve unhelpful patterns or stagnant energy. Trust in the process and allow the Flame to work its magic. If any emotions arise, let them come up to be witnessed and felt as they move through you.

8. Stay here for as long as you feel called to do so. This is your time to absorb the Violet Flame's essence and energy deeply. Simply be present, feeling the gentle yet powerful waves of transformation taking place within you.

9. As you feel ready to complete your practice, take a moment to express gratitude. Gratitude helps solidify the energetic work you've done and honors the presence of the Violet Flame.

10. Begin to bring your awareness back to your physical surroundings. Feel the ground beneath you, the air on your skin,

and the gentle rhythm of your breath. Allow yourself to return to the present moment, while still carrying the energy of the Violet Flame within.

After your practice, take some time to reflect. How do you feel? What sensations, thoughts, or emotions came up during the process? Did you feel any specific areas of your body reacting to the Violet Flame's energy? These reflections are important as they help you become more aware of the subtle shifts happening within you.

Journaling allows you to record your experiences and recognize patterns over time. You might note down any visions, sensations, or intuitive messages that came to you during the practice. Keeping a record of your experiences can help deepen your connection to the Violet Flame and provide guidance for future practices.

Regular practice is key to strengthening your connection with the Violet Flame. As you continue to work with this energy, its transformative impact will become more obvious in your life. Aim to integrate this practice into your daily routine, even if only for a few minutes each day. The more you connect with the Violet Flame, the more it will assist with your growth and expansion.

CHAPTER 2

Keepers of the Flame

'I burn throughout eternity,'
the Violet Flame shared with me. 'And like any fire,
I burn brighter when I am tended to.'

'Who tends to this fire?' I asked.
'Who stands as guardian to something so sacred?'

The Violet Flame swirled its multidimensional,
fractal-like fire all around me: 'The Keepers of the Flame:
They are a group of souls who have transcended
the confines of form, assisting those who have forgotten
to tend to the Violet Flame. These Keepers do not seek
your worship, their presence is a gift, a reminder of what
you already are. The wisdom, the unconditional love,
the courage they hold – it is within you, too.
They are not separate from you.
They are an aspect of you.
Just as I am an aspect of you, too.'

In that moment, I understood.
We are always supported.

There is a group of etheric beings who are entrusted as the Keepers of the Violet Flame. They have transcended this physical realm and now exist in higher-vibrational dimensions and planes of existence that are free of form. They are ascended masters, angels, and star beings who are all working together to serve as the Violet Flame's custodians.

Within this book I've chosen to share with you six Keepers of the Flame who I have a personal connection with. These are St Germain and Lady Portia, Yeshua and Mary Magdalene, Archangel Zadkiel and Holy Amethyst. However, there are other beings who are connected to the Violet Flame across many traditions (for example, Goddess Tara and her counterpart, the bodhisattva Avalokiteshvara), so I also encourage you to explore beyond the pages of this book to find which of the Keepers feel most resonant to you and your path or lineage, if any.

What is the purpose of the Keepers of the Flame? These benevolent beings work in harmony with humanity to support us as we move through this period of accelerated awakening. They are revered as guardians of esoteric wisdom, silently working behind the veils of the material world, acting as a bridge to channel the potent energy of the Violet Flame, and bringing its wisdom forth to Earth. The Keepers are constantly working as guides and teachers for those who seek to unlock the mysteries of the Violet Flame, to be able to use it for personal transformation, spiritual evolution, and healing.

As the Violet Flame aids us in finding balance between the internal masculine and feminine energies, so too, the Keepers of the Flame are beings who come in pairs: Both a masculine and a feminine counterpart to represent polarity and symbolize the concept of coming into wholeness through divine union.

These Keepers of the Flame each represent certain traits that can support us in navigating through life from that place of universal love. The reason they're being shared is to support you in understanding what the Violet Flame represents and the archetypal energies you can embody as a result of working with the Flame.

It's always key to remember that any ascended masters or deities are symbolic of what we already hold within. So, it's crucial not to outsource our power to them in any way or worship anything outside of ourselves. Connecting with these beings serves as a poignant reminder that we inherently possess all these qualities already and they're able to be harnessed. Like these beings, we too, are guardians of the Violet Flame.

The Etheric Custodians
Saint Germain and Lady Portia

The couple most widely known as Keepers of the Violet Flame are ascended masters. Their union is seen as a divine partnership, forged through their complementary energies.

Though their union isn't based on historical accounts, their meeting is said to have occurred in the celestial planes, where their shared dedication to the principles of transformation, mercy, and spiritual alchemy united them.

Saint Germain, the master alchemist, represents wisdom, freedom, and a reminder of the transformative impact that spiritual practices can have on us when done consistently. Lady Portia embodies purification, intuitive guidance, and nurturing protection. Together, their energies create a powerful symbiosis that magnifies the transformational power of the Violet Flame, bringing balance and harmony to those who invoke its energy.

In one of Saint Germain's incarnations on Earth, he was said to turn base metals into gold. This symbolizes the literal transformation of metals, and also the concept of inner alchemy – transmuting one's spiritual and mental state from a metaphorical 'lead' to a metaphorical 'gold' of deeper consciousness.

He is a harbinger of the Age of Aquarius, which is a time of spiritual awakening and expanded awareness. He is a guardian of esoteric wisdom, promoting principles of love, unity, and spiritual evolution. Often, Saint Germain's messages focus on the interconnectedness of all beings and the importance of cultivating love and harmony among humanity. He supports us in harmonizing and transforming denser emotions by steering us toward the alchemical process where we can use the energy and shape it into something else. This gives the opportunity to transmute the heavier emotions we're feeling into a more progressive energy, so we're able to expand. Through this process, we can uncover the gift that lies within the shadow, and this becomes the road map for moving forward.

The Aquarian Age

The Age of Aquarius, of which Saint Germain is the leader, describes a profound shift in collective consciousness. In astrology, it marks humanity's transition from the dense structures and hierarchical focus of the Age of Pisces, where value was placed on money, power, and control, into a time characterized by innovation, community, and spiritual awakening. Ruled by Uranus, the planet of revolution and higher consciousness, Aquarius carries the energy of liberation, individuality, progressive thinking, and a deep connection to the collective whole. This era invites us to break free from outdated systems, embrace equality, and cocreate a world grounded in love, compassion, and unity. In the Age of Aquarius we move out from the energy of 'me' and into an energy of 'we' as the illusion of separation dissolves.

Lady Portia is a goddess of divine justice who embodies virtues of compassion, mercy, and forgiveness. She oversees the workings of karmic and cosmic law to bring about divine order. In this role, she's seen as a guardian of moral and spiritual integrity, ensuring the equilibrium of energies within the universe. Her presence brings forth clarity and fairness and assists us in bringing conscious awareness to the universal laws that govern the spiritual realms.

She's often depicted as a being of grace and compassion, offering guidance and support to anyone seeking balance and harmony in their lives. As a divine feminine archetype, she represents the nurturing and compassionate aspects of spiritual growth, fostering inner peace and understanding. Her gentle presence supports us in our quest for inner truth and a life founded on justice. Through the lens of cosmic law, she assists individuals in exploring the depths of their own hearts to discover the authenticity of their inner truth. Through her, we can learn to align our actions with principles of justice, kindness, and compassion, fostering a life rich in morals and integrity.

Yeshua and Mary Magdalene

Yeshua (or Jesus Christ, as he's known in Christianity) and Mary Magdalene are also Keepers of the Violet Flame. They walked this Earth together in sacred union, spreading the word of universal love. Mary Magdalene was the human embodiment of the divine feminine, and Yeshua was the human embodiment of the divine masculine. When they came together, they created the 'whole,' returning to become one with 'God,' and it was from this place they were able to perform miracles.

Mary Magdalene, the feminine guide, channel, and oracle, brought through the messages of divine universal love. Yeshua was the masculine leader and carried this message out to the world to show people the light they hold within and for all. Together, Mary Magdalene and Yeshua are revered as Keepers of the Violet Flame, since their mission on Earth was to guide humanity back to its truest vibration of universal love and union.

Through her unwavering devotion to Yeshua, Mary Magdalene epitomizes unconditional love. Her willingness to stand by him, even amidst adversity, during crucifixion and burial, demonstrates a profound commitment. Through her devotion, Magdalene teaches the importance of surrendering to the divine plan and living a life of service.

She also embodies sovereignty. Despite any distortions that have been passed down through time, she was a woman of influence and independence, defying societal constraints to follow her own spiritual path. Her relationship with Yeshua illustrates her capacity to assert her sovereignty and embrace her divine purpose, inspiring others to reclaim their autonomy and spiritual sovereignty, too.

Magdalene's journey also represents a powerful narrative of reclamation – of reclaiming her identity, her womb, and her voice. Despite historical mischaracterizations (for example, in the Bible she was depicted as a sinner, a prostitute possessed by demons, until Jesus came and saved her soul), alternative truths are being uncovered about Magdalene and she is now more widely viewed as a spiritual guide who walked by Yeshua's side as his equal.

As the divine feminine energy rises during this current global awakening, more and more people are connecting with what they feel to be the truth of who Mary Magdalene was, outside of biblical teachings. This is a restoration of her rightful place in sacred narratives, for her to be seen and heard. Her story inspires individuals to reclaim their own narratives, heal from societal judgments, and embrace their inherent worth.

In the Bible, Yeshua is referred to as 'The Light of the World,' and is often shown holding a flame in the palm of his hand, known as the Christ Light. This is also believed to be the Violet

Flame – Yeshua was the vibration of the Violet Flame as he was able to practice alchemy. The Bible tells of him turning water into wine and feeding thousands of people with just five loaves of bread and two fish. With the light he held (the Violet Flame), he performed what people perceived to be miracles, such as healing the sick and walking on water.

Despite his divine nature, Yeshua exemplifies humility in his teachings and actions. He lived a humble life, choosing simplicity and service over power and riches. Yeshua washed the feet of his disciples to show that when in true service to the whole, there is no hierarchy. His example teaches us to cultivate inner humility and genuine compassion toward others and the importance of unity, connection, and equality.

Yeshua embodies the essence of service through his selfless dedication to humanity. He devoted his life to ministering to the marginalized and uplifting the oppressed. He taught that true greatness comes from serving others and urged his followers to love their neighbors as themselves. His life of service inspires individuals to embrace compassionate action and work toward the betterment of humanity.

Yeshua exemplifies radical forgiveness: his message was to forgive others, as through this we free ourselves and can fully experience universal love. His ultimate act of forgiveness is symbolized by the cross, where he was said to pray for his persecutors and extended divine mercy to all humanity.

Archangel Zadkiel and Holy Amethyst

Archangel Zadkiel and Holy Amethyst are deeply connected through their roles in the angelic realm, being the angels associated with the Violet Flame. Their connection is characterized by their joint mission to assist humanity in purifying and elevating us toward unity consciousness. Their connection through the Violet Flame is synergistic, meaning that their combined energies amplify the Flame's power.

Archangel Zadkiel is known for helping us work through karma. He plays a crucial role in assisting individuals to understand that their timelines shift as a result of their actions and the importance of making choices from love over fear. He assists souls in learning from past experiences, facilitating the karmic lessons that promote spiritual growth and evolution.

Another virtue associated with Archangel Zadkiel is that of mercy. Like Yeshua, he teaches the compassionate forgiveness we can give to ourselves or others. Zadkiel's energy encourages the release of judgments and resentments and awakens the soul to the liberating power of forgiveness. This divine mercy is a coming to acceptance, an active force that transforms and heals, breaking the chains of denser emotions and thoughts that bind individuals to their past mistakes. He stands for integrity and inspires individuals to live in their truth, aligning thoughts, words, and actions with their highest spiritual values. This alignment fosters a life of authenticity and honor, where decisions are made from a place of wisdom and integrity.

Purification is at the core of Holy Amethyst's essence. She assists in the cleansing of our spiritual, emotional, mental, and physical spaces, using the Violet Flame. She illuminates shadows by shining a light on old patterns, beliefs, and energies from which we're ready to evolve.

Holy Amethyst is intimately connected with the power of intuition, guiding us to trust our inner knowing and to navigate our spiritual path with clarity. Intuition is our soul's language, and Holy Amethyst enhances this divine communication, enabling us to receive and interpret intuitive messages. Her energy helps to clear the mental clutter that can cloud our judgment, allowing our insights to come forth with clarity and purpose. Holy Amethyst's energy also symbolizes divine protection. She's like a sanctuary, offering a protective shield around those who call upon her. This is to maintain the integrity of our energy field. In a world where we're surrounded by external influences, her protection assists us in discernment and viewing through the lens of love. Holy Amethyst teaches us that protection is about creating harmony within.

Becoming a Keeper of the Flame

Through this meditation practice, you'll connect with the etheric beings known as Keepers of the Violet Flame: Saint Germain, Lady Portia, Yeshua, Mary Magdalene, Archangel Zadkiel, and Holy Amethyst. You will also initiate yourself as a Keeper of the Flame. This is to deepen your connection to the Flame before you begin to call upon it more frequently in the following chapters.

1. Find a quiet, comfortable space where you won't be disturbed. You may choose to light a violet candle or hold a piece of amethyst as a physical representation of the Violet Flame.

Sit or lie down comfortably, taking a few deep breaths to center yourself.

2. Begin by grounding and centering yourself. Imagine strong roots extending from the base of your spine or feet, anchoring you deeply into the earth. Feel the stability and support of the earth beneath you. As you breathe in, draw up this grounding energy, and as you exhale, let go of any tension and surrender to being held by the earth.

3. Imagine a bright violet light surrounding you as you become the center of this purifying flame. Sit with the Violet Flame and feel it gently vibrating through your cells and expanding out into your auric field. Here you can repeat the invocation from Chapter 1, Invoking the Flame (*Connecting to the Violet Flame, step 5, page 19*), if you feel called to do so.

4. Now imagine yourself standing before the Temple of the Violet Flame. The temple is a magnificent structure, radiating a soft, violet glow that beckons you closer. The air is filled with sweet, calming scents of lavender, frankincense, and rose, creating an atmosphere of peace and tranquility. There are two huge amethyst crystal geodes framing the entrance to this temple.

5. As you step forward, you feel the cool, smooth stone of the temple's steps beneath your feet. With each step, you feel more grounded and supported. Quartz crystal doors, adorned with intricate carvings, slowly swing open inviting you into a sacred space filled with loving energy.

6. Upon entering, you find yourself in a vast, circular chamber. The walls are adorned with beautiful murals depicting scenes of transformation, union, and purity all bathed in a soft, violet light emanating from the center of the room. The atmosphere is

peaceful, and you can feel the vibrational resonance of the Violet Flame holding you. There are clear quartz points throughout the temple creating prisms for light to move through and leaving rainbow droplets all around the space. As you walk deeper into the temple, you notice a vibrant Violet Flame flickering in the center. It dances gracefully, casting a light that illuminates the walls. This Flame represents the heart of the temple, a source of purification, transformation, and universal love.

7. Take a moment to stand before this radiant flame. Feel its warmth enveloping you, wrapping you in a cocoon of love and grace. You know this is a safe space where you can acknowledge old patterns, move through emotion, heal through the awareness of new templates forming, and connect to your own inner light. Allow yourself to absorb the energy of the Flame, letting it fill you with a sense of surrender.

8. As you stand in the Temple of the Violet Flame, you become aware that you're not alone. The Keepers of the Violet Flame are gathering around you gracefully, each embodying unique qualities and energies that you hold within and will support you on your journey.

9. First, **Saint Germain** steps forward, his presence exuding strength and wisdom. The master alchemist Saint Germain is here to guide you in transforming challenges into opportunities for growth. As he approaches, you feel his energy resonating with your own. 'Welcome, courageous soul,' he says warmly. 'Embrace the alchemy of your life. Every challenge you face is an invitation to grow, to expand, and to transform your experiences into wisdom.' Allow Saint Germain's words to sink in. Visualize the challenges in your life as raw materials waiting

to be transformed. Imagine them shifting and changing in the violet light, becoming opportunities for growth and healing.

10. Next, **Lady Portia** emerges, radiating grace and balance. She represents divine justice and harmony, and her energy surrounds you like a soft embrace. 'You are deserving of balance and harmony in your life,' she reminds you. 'Release any fear that disrupts your peace. Trust that you are supported and everything is unfolding for your highest good.' Feel Lady Portia's nurturing energy flowing through you. Imagine any imbalances in your life being gently resolved as you stand in her presence.

11. Then, **Yeshua** steps forward, emanating a powerful, all-encompassing love. His heart glows brightly, enveloping you in warmth and compassion. 'Feel my love surrounding you,' he whispers. 'You are never alone in your journey. You are cherished and loved beyond measure. Remember, your capacity for forgiveness, compassion, and universal love is infinite. You are pure of heart.' Allow this all-encompassing love to wash over you, melting away anything that's keeping you from knowing your worth. Imagine it filling your heart, expanding outward until you feel completely enveloped in divine love.

12. Next, **Mary Magdalene** approaches, her presence embodying the divine feminine. 'You are a sovereign being,' she tells you, encouraging you to embrace your inner power. 'Honor your intuition and trust in your unique path. You do have choice, and you have the strength to overcome any obstacle that stands in your way. Use your voice and speak your truth.' As Mary Magdalene speaks, visualize yourself standing tall in your power. Feel the confidence radiating from your core, knowing that you're equipped to navigate your journey with grace and purpose.

13. Finally, **Archangel Zadkiel** and **Holy Amethyst** appear, their combined energies amplifying your truth and integrity. They're here to assist you in purifying your path and removing anything that doesn't serve your truth. 'You are safe to express,' they say in unison. 'We are here to help you create space for your true essence to shine and your full expression to be felt.' Feel their loving energy holding you and imagine the Violet Flame purifying your being, leaving you feeling lighter, brighter, and more at peace.

14. With the presence of these beings surrounding you, visualize the radiant Violet Flame igniting in your palms. Feel its warmth and the tingles as it fills your hands with light. Bring your palms together and place them over your heart, feeling the energy flow between them.

15. Take a moment to state your intention to become a Keeper of the Violet Flame. This intention is a powerful declaration of your devotion to personal growth and your contribution to the collective healing of the world. You may choose to speak this affirmation or write your own:

> With an open heart, I now proclaim,
> I am a Keeper of the Violet Flame.
> With this Flame, I embrace my role,
> to liberate myself and heal the whole.
> I harness this energy, my intention pure,
> for the highest good, of that, I am sure.
> In unity and love, we rise again,
> I am a Keeper of the Violet Flame.

As you voice your intention, feel the acceptance and support of the Keepers. They surround you with love, acknowledging your commitment, and inviting you to create a circle with them.

16. Now, take a few moments in meditation to allow any intuitive messages to come through. In this meditative state, you may receive insights, images, or feelings. Perhaps you see symbols or colors, hear whispers of wisdom, or simply feel a sense of knowing. Trust whatever arises, observing it without judgment or over-analysis. This is a gift from the Keepers, guiding you on your journey.

17. As you connect more deeply with the Flame, imagine it radiating outward from your heart, creating a sphere of violet light around you. This sphere is a shield, which reminds you of the resilience, courage, and strength you hold. Within this sphere, you're free to explore your true potential.

18. Once your journey to the Temple of the Violet Flame feels complete, take a moment to express your gratitude to the Keepers for their guidance and support. Thank them for the wisdom and love they've shared with you. Know that you can return to this sacred space whenever you wish, and the Keepers will always be here to welcome your return.

19. Begin to walk out of the Temple of the Violet Flame, back through the doorway you entered through. Gradually bring your awareness to the present moment and the room you're currently in. Take a few deep breaths, feeling the surface beneath you, and the air around you. Visualize the Violet Flame gently receding inward, shrinking down, while still gently flickering in the center of your heart space.

20. When you feel ready, open your eyes and return to your day, feeling grounded and centered. You may wish to take a moment to journal your experiences, insights, or feelings from this meditation. Writing can help you integrate the messages you received and reinforce your connection with the Violet Flame.

CHAPTER 3

Illuminating Shadows

'This flame does not ask for perfection.
Perfection is illusion,' the Violet Flame roared to me.
'I do ask for courage. The courage to face the shadows within,
for you to unearth the pieces that you have buried deep,
to stand naked before the truth of who you are.'

I trembled before its radiant fire.
'What if I'm not ready?' I whispered.
'What if the darkness consumes me?'

'Step into the fire,' the Violet Flame urged.
'This flame is not here to destroy you,
it is here to transform you.
Burn away the false masks,
the stories that no longer serve you.
Do not fear the unveiling of your shadow,
as it is the gateway to your light.
You cannot outrun your shadows, for they are
the parts of you that require acknowledgment.
When you can accept and integrate them,
you can love them back into the light
and in doing so, you'll find the liberation you seek.'

I knew it was time to face the parts of me I had
been hiding from. To honor every shadow,
and to trust that within this violet fire,
I would find my freedom.

When the Violet Flame comes into your life, the first thing it will do is shine a light on all parts of the Self that are preventing you from embodying universal love. It will highlight your shadow aspects: the 'shadow' being anything that can create an emotional reaction to a situation that stems from a place of limiting beliefs, a lack mentality, or deeply ingrained fears. As a result, it manifests more of these denser experiences as like energy attracts like energy.

When we're triggered or confronted by life's challenges, the Violet Flame can be the light we call upon to feel guided and supported in moments of shadow. Shadow work is about acknowledging the parts of us around which we may feel judgment, and instead, to integrate them through awareness and acceptance. The Violet Flame offers us the perspective to see our shadows as invitations for growth, as opportunities to reclaim the parts of ourselves we've been avoiding, pushing away, shaming, or rejecting, consciously or subconsciously. It assists us in seeing clearly so we're able to navigate the triggers, choose to change the way we respond and, therefore, interrupt our previous patterns to transform the outcome. This results in us beginning to create a new reality for ourselves, as our external world starts to shift with the Violet Flame lighting the way.

The frequency of creation is universal love.

The result of creation is abundance.

We do not actually have to create love and abundance in our lives, it's always present.

We just create the limitations when it comes to being able to access it – that is the shadow.

Trust the Trigger

Triggers are our teachers. They are certain situations, people, or places that create a dense emotional response or reaction within us, such as fear, anger, pain, agitation, unease, or upset. More often than not, we react this way because there's an unresolved issue that's still playing out in our subconscious mind.

When we're triggered, it brings up the shadow aspects of our being. Parts of ourselves that are often hidden away within our psyche. Attributes that have been shamed, neglected, repressed, or pushed away and avoided. They can also be the voices of someone else or societal conditioning that's imprinted false beliefs about us or the world around us. These shadows, programs, and beliefs over time create a veil of illusion that can hold us in a cycle of lack mentality, keeping us small and living in fear. When we reside in the shadow frequency, potential suffering can be experienced, and we slip into victim patterns: The type of patterning where we disempower ourselves by choosing to find and place blame on everything and everyone else, feeling as if the world is working against us.

Now, when I speak of fear, I mean something different to that of our primal instincts. The use of the word 'fear' in the English language has created some confusion and people often put feelings of fear and primal instincts in the same category. Instincts are a survival technique to ensure we run from predators, and they support us in differentiating between safe situations and dangerous ones. Essentially, they are primal reactions brought on by a threat to our safety and they kick in to keep us alive.

However, most of the fears we feel are created through illusions that program us to feel we're lacking. These illusions then restrict or disempower us in some way. We can't eliminate our instincts (nor would we want to), however, we can transmute fear.

Fear = False Evidence Appearing Real

One thing I've learned from my own healing journey is that often, within spiritual or healing ceremonies, rituals, and practices, there can be a focus on releasing parts of ourselves that 'are not serving us.' However, this is still self-rejection, where we discard certain elements that have been or are present in our lives, pushing them to one side. Energy doesn't just cease to exist, so we can do all the release rituals we want, but if we haven't faced off with our shadow, it will still persist. It will still be lurking in the dark corners of our consciousness, ready to bite us when we least expect it!

It's important for us first to feel, and then move through, our painful emotions, transforming the energy so we can access the gift awaiting us on the other side. Ultimately, what our triggers show us is where we need to practice unconditional love for ourselves. Shadows only continue to exist when there is something blocking the light; either through complete unawareness or by being suppressed, ignored, shamed, and rejected. The key to transforming these shadows is by bringing them out into the open. We do this through acknowledgment, awareness, self-honesty, and transparency. The Violet Flame is the catalyst for this, for when we call on the Violet Flame, we're asking to shine a light on our shadows so they have nowhere to hide.

Of course, the decision to journey into the shadowy depths takes courage. It takes effort to bring ourselves into a place of conscious awareness so that we can observe our habits and reflect on why we behave or react to life the way we do. It can also be confronting, as it demands complete honesty. When doing this work, there are no excuses; it involves taking radical responsibility for yourself and your circumstances. We begin to shift from a disempowered state of 'the world is working against me,' to a more empowered perspective of 'this is showing me something.' This is one of the ways the Violet Flame's energy of transformation can assist us. We can't always control what's happening but we can change and transform the way we respond to it.

When we're triggered, we notice certain feelings arising for us. Emotion is energy in motion, so it needs to move through us in some way, which is why we can end up reacting to triggers from an emotionally charged space. However, the more we become aware of this, the more we can acknowledge our thoughts and feelings, then breathe through the emotion as it moves through us instead of reacting. Really, what the emotion requires more than anything is to be acknowledged and felt.

This is where the Violet Flame really supports us. Instead of getting caught up in a whirlwind of destructive emotion, we can take a pause and give ourselves space, calling on the Violet Flame to hold us and assist with the alchemizing process. Here, we can allow ourselves to acknowledge and feel what is arising, then choose to become the observer. By becoming more conscious of the emotion and what it's showing us, we can expand our awareness and unravel a deeper understanding of where the core of the fear, belief, or conditioning started.

This is where the trigger really starts to teach us, as it leads us back to the place where the root of the unresolved issue began. We then begin to practice acceptance, love, and compassion for our shadow self so we can integrate it fully. When you start to do this, it leads to liberation because there's nothing that can take hold of you when you're viewing life through the lens of universal love. You don't have anything to run from or avoid. You don't find yourself perpetuating drama. When you can face yourself in truth, you can then face anything life throws at you.

> *'The degree to which a person can grow is directly proportional to the amount of truth they can accept about themselves without running away.'*
> LELAND VAL VAN DE WALL

Trusting Your Triggers to Teach

In this practice, we will deepen self-awareness by calling on the Violet Flame to shine a light on the times in your life when you were triggered and an undesired outcome was created. Through honest, compassionate contemplation and inquiry, you will begin to recognize the behavioral patterns that you want to grow from and transform them into wisdom. Through having a deeper awareness of your triggers you can reclaim your power.

1. Find a quiet and comfortable space where you can be without distraction. Light a candle to represent the Violet Flame. Take a few deep breaths, allowing yourself to be grounded and centered in the present moment. (*You can revisit the Invoking the Flame practice on page 15 for more in-depth preparation and grounding exercises.*)

2. Gently bring your awareness to the type of events and relationships in your life that cause you to feel disempowered or lead you into the blame game. Ask the Violet Flame to shine a light on to these for you, so you can see them clearly. For example:

   ✦ Are there any relationships in which you feel you abandon your own needs to keep others happy or avoid conflict?

   ✦ When challenges arise, do you ever catch yourself thinking you're without a choice or feel you have little influence over the outcome?

   ✦ What type of events cause this feeling?

- What beliefs surface when you think about times you've felt disempowered?

- What type of situations lead you to either finding fault through blame or coming up with excuses?

3. Allow yourself to acknowledge and witness these patterns honestly, without judgment or reliving the experience. The intention here is not to re-experience the emotions they stirred in you, but simply to recognize the patterns that exist. In this practice, you're stepping into the role of an observer, looking at the situations as though you're reviewing them from a distance, with clarity and neutrality.

4. If you notice the emotional intensity building or if you find yourself slipping back into the story of the experience, gently acknowledge this. Pause and take a few deep breaths. Reconnect to the Violet Flame and focus on the breath moving in and out of your body and ground yourself back into the present. This helps you return to a state of observation rather than reaction. (Sometimes, stepping away from the practice momentarily can be supportive, so take a break if you need to and return once you can witness these memories as an observer.)

5. Take out your journal or a pen and paper, and write down your reflections on the following questions:

    - What are the recurring triggers, events, relationships, or patterns in my life that lead me into disempowerment or needing to place blame?

    - How do these triggers and patterns disempower me and keep me caught in cycles of perceived suffering?

- What are these triggers teaching me about myself and my shadow aspects?

- What deeper truths or lessons lie beneath these triggers and patterns?

If you feel challenged to answer these reflections, take a moment to be with the Violet Flame. See it illuminating the answers and bringing them into your awareness.

6. Close your eyes and visualize yourself standing before a beautiful mirror reflecting back the truth of your being. As you gaze into this mirror, allow the triggers and shadow aspects you identified during the reflective inquiry surface within your awareness again. Witness them with compassion and curiosity, acknowledging the lessons they hold for you.

7. Begin to visualize the Violet Flame surrounding you and the mirror, bringing light. With an open heart and gentle acceptance, recognize that these shadow aspects are not flaws or weaknesses – there's nothing here to be shamed. They are invitations for growth and transformation, and no matter the depths of those shadows, know at your core you are universal love. Spend as much time as you need bringing love to these shadow aspects as they're brought into the light. If you like, you can also call on the Keepers of the Flame to support you in this embracing of your shadows.

8. Acknowledge the shadow aspects and affirm:

> *'You hold no power over me.*
> *With the Violet Flame I set myself free.'*

9. Feel the Violet Flame burning away threads of disempowerment and transforming them into newfound wisdom, which comes from having a deeper understanding of yourself. Conclude by giving gratitude to the trigger, for what it teaches you.

10. Finish the practice by holding the Violet Flame in your heart and feeling the light filling you, grounding you back to the here and now.

Commit to calling on the Violet Flame whenever you feel you're in moments of trigger so it can illuminate the shadow aspect that's felt scared, fearful, lacking, or limited in some way. Reclaim your power and bring the shadow into the light, as it's a part of you that needs to be acknowledged and loved.

Unlock the Gift

Often, beyond our greatest shadow lies our greatest gift. So where there's resistance in life, you can almost always guarantee that growth and expansion await on the other side. From this journey so far, we know that our shadow aspects usually create a subconscious reaction to life that causes us perceived suffering. It keeps us in a loop of feeling disempowered or playing a blame game that's rooted in fear and lack.

When we consciously bring awareness to our triggers and then integrate them through bringing them into the light, we can identify the gift waiting on the other side of the shadow. This gift is usually something we have to offer to the world, and it's the bridge to reaching the polarity of the shadow self – which is our most authentic expression.

I love to look at this process like a beautiful rainbow:

- The rain that pours down is the emotional response to a trigger.

- The sun coming out to shine is the awareness and lessons learnt from observing the trigger.

- The rainbow is the gift we find within the lesson, the bridge to our true essence.

When we understand the truth of who we are and don't react to life from the shadow, we can live from a place of authenticity; that's the never-ending pot of gold at the end of the rainbow, bringing pure abundance into our lives.

✦

One of the most triggering scenarios for me is having my picture taken by a photographer. Over the last few years, I've been invited to lean into this area of growth with photo shoots presenting themselves. There was one such shoot with a photographer who'd photographed many prestigious events, celebrities, and musicians. (Talk about throwing myself in at the deep end.) It was one of the most profoundly triggering situations I'd found myself in for a long time.

I prepared myself for the shoot. I had some beautiful clothes to wear and on entering the space, I was feeling good. I looked in the mirror, smiled, and I mouthed to myself 'I love you.' I could feel a flutter of excitement in anticipation of how the next few hours would unfold. As the photographer was setting up, I mentioned to him that I can be quite nervous in front of a camera. He was gentle and assured me there were no expectations, that we were going to allow flow.

The set constructed, we began. I walked into the center of a black backdrop, with two massive bright lights shining straight on me. Almost immediately, that flutter of excitement turned into panic as I realized there was nothing else there but me. I felt exposed and vulnerable. The photographer began to take photos and, immediately, the critic in my mind arose.

My inner dialogue was loud:

> *Every inch of my physical body is being observed right now. Through a lens. Do I look too big? Am I tensing? I forgot to check my hair, is my hair OK? Am I being judged right now? I wonder what the photographer is thinking. What if I look disgusting? Am I disgusting? Am I breathing?! Shit, I'm holding my breath. Just breathe! You need to breathe to look relaxed. Oh no, my face, I forgot about my face... am I frowning?*

Within the first 30 seconds, I was already exhausted. Yet I felt a sense of determination: *I can do this; I can overcome this discomfort.*

Sensing my unease, the photographer gently tried to guide me. I wasn't responding to his direction and he thought I wasn't listening to him. What he didn't know was that my inner dialogue was so loud, I could barely hear him. My mind had become a showroom of shouty voices and I was trying to zone them out so I could hear what he was saying. Plus, he was almost invisible, sinking into the dark background behind the glaring light in front of me.

From that moment on, every time the camera clicked it was like a part of my self-esteem was being chipped away from me. As the photo shoot continued, I knew I was frozen, petrified of getting it wrong.

Then the defeatist thoughts seeped in. The *'I can't do this'* bricks began building a staircase around my heart, creating an escape route out of this realm. Going into a spiral of internal criticism, the only successful movement was that of metaphorically running up those stairs until I'd reached a point of disembodiment. Violet was vacant. At least it's safe there.

Completely zoned out from my current situation, my mind reached silence. Floating in the void I felt the light of the Violet Flame reminding me that this was not my true essence, and it gently grounded me back down. Now fully present once more, I sat in silence against the black backdrop, the room in total darkness, the bright studio light directly in front of me.

In this moment I became aware of the paradox of light and dark that was simultaneously playing out, here in this experience. I was there with the brightest of lights shining right at me. Darkness was present but this powerful spotlight was keeping it at bay. I realized that it's only when our inner light dims that darkness can really take its hold.

In that blinding light, I saw clearly. I recalled why I was doing the photo shoot, for the possibility of what it could be. For the opportunity to overcome my resistance and receive the *gift* of liberation. For the expansion that comes from living life outside your comfort zone. I remembered that I have the Violet Flame here with me, ready to transform any situation. I felt my soul speaking, which never gives up hope.

Some say you shouldn't look for the possibilities within a situation and only act upon 'what is.' Some say the concept of 'hope' is one that takes us out of trust or knowing. That it can be 'wishful thinking.'

I ask, what is a life without hope?

Hope is a part of us that believes, and knows, it can be; that positive outcomes will prevail even amidst the trials, tribulations, and uncertainties of the physical world. This kind of hope is not merely wishful thinking, it's the type that's anchored in the faith that there is a purpose and meaning to human existence, beyond what's visible or immediately understandable.

Right there in that hope you'll find the Violet Flame. It's there to guide us through change, to help us evolve. It's the studio light in a dark room, shining against a black backdrop. It's our inner light that can never fade out. This was the teaching that came from the trigger. With this realization, I remembered my truth. I channeled that hope and felt the Violet Flame burning from within, as bright as the studio light... THIS WAS THE GIFT!

With the gift integrated, remembering my essence, reclaiming my truth, and with the Violet Flame burning within, I asked the photographer for a break. I took a moment to be with myself outside the room, and the version of me who had begun the photo shoot with an 'I love you,' was here. I felt Mary Magdalene with me, her grace and all-encompassing love.

When I returned, we finished the shoot. I became gentle with myself, and I changed that inner dialogue to words of encouragement and empowerment, so I began to smile from the inside out. As I left, I felt it had been a beautiful experience and something special had been created. This was the gift that was unlocked through the trigger – connecting to the hope in my heart and remembering the inner beauty I carry – leading me to self-compassion. In the process, it also gave me profound insights, integrating the parts of myself that were rooted in unworthiness and transforming those shadow beliefs into love.

A few weeks later, the photographer sent me some of the images he'd taken. I felt emotional receiving them. I saw myself clearly. There I was. All of myself was present in the photos: the me who was anxious, the me who was vulnerable, the me who was challenged, the me who persevered, the me who embraced the fullness of life, the me who finished the shoot feeling unconditionally loving toward myself and the experience. A full cycle of transformation was present in the picture with the Violet Flame flickering in my heart. I felt liberated.

Conscious Change

It's with conscious awareness that we can choose our perspective, which means we can also change the way we respond to life and effectively reshape our entire reality. Because with every thought, feeling, and action, we're shaping the world around us. This is where transformation is birthed from – the moment we choose differently. To reprogram our shadow tendencies, it takes commitment to practicing awareness and applying the lessons, so that we can reside in the gift frequency to embody truth fully. We have to first observe, to understand mindfully, so we can experience the gift and then it becomes our life.

As explained earlier in this chapter, our shadow most obviously rears its head when someone, or something, has noticeably triggered us. However, it also slowly and subtly seeps out during day-to-day life. When our shadows play out in this way, it's more nuanced and can be more challenging to spot, as there's not been a specific event that's led to a more intense emotional reaction. Instead, it's known through the seemingly unimportant things that almost go unnoticed. It's also the inner dialogue of our ego mind and thoughts that can continuously drip-feed our shadow.

When I started calling on the Violet Flame to shine a light upon my shadows, I noticed my internal narrator would sometimes take on the voice of a 'mean girl' who'd criticize and tell me off whenever I did something 'wrong.'

For example, if I accidentally dropped something on the floor, she'd say words along the lines of 'Argh, you idiot!' The crazy thing is I'd never speak to anyone else like that, yet it was normal for me to speak to myself in that way. Even crazier, this was so normal that I didn't even notice half the time that I was speaking to myself in a derogatory way because it was such a regular occurrence.

It may not seem like a big deal, but all these little words of discouragement or negativity do have an effect on our energy and self-esteem, as the subconscious mind doesn't miss a thing. These nuanced shadows playing out over time mean they're slowly creating a belief within us. That's how programming works, with repetition and consistency. Once these are installed as subconscious beliefs, we can find that when big opportunities come up, we've created a barrier, and it holds us back from truly experiencing what life has to offer.

When I became aware of my more nuanced shadows playing out, I then realized how much of my inner world was speaking from fear, lack, or belittling myself...

- 'I can't afford to do that.'
- 'Gosh, I look so tired today.'
- 'Nobody cares about what I have to say.'
- 'I always mess things up.'

With every word or thought that we speak, we're shaping our current reality and creating our future. Words are a group of letters put together to create meaning, and what is that referred to as? *Spelling*. There's the clue. Our words are our spells... What do you want to create?

I remember my own moment of realization, that I can experience both Heaven and Hell here on Earth and I get to *choose*. I get to choose how I perceive what is happening and how I respond.

> *'Your mind will always believe everything you tell it. Feed it hope, feed it love, feed it truth.'*
> UNKNOWN

It begins with the words and thoughts that we start choosing. Anything that's been learned can be un-learned. Anything that's been programmed can be reprogrammed, and where there's an old belief, we can shift into new beliefs. This is transformation, this is the magic of the Violet Flame.

Choosing Change

In this practice, we'll embark on an exploration of conscious choice, as we observe and transmute our shadow thought patterns. Through the gentle alchemy of awareness and compassion, we'll rewrite the narratives, change the story, and embrace a reality infused with empowerment. Ultimately, choosing change forges the pathway to liberation.

1. When you wake up, begin your day with the intention to cultivate self-awareness, and from this moment, you choose change. Visualize a radiant Violet Flame surrounding you – it acts as a grounding force that will be there to support you in illuminating the shadows throughout your day so you can see clearly where choosing love is necessary.

2. All day, remain observant of your passing thoughts, especially those tinged with fear, lack, or doubt. Notice when you catch yourself engaging in unkind self-talk or an inner dialogue rooted in lack and limitation. Whenever you identify a shadow thought, gently note it down in a journal or on your phone, along with the feeling it's creating within you and the false belief it's affirming. For example:

    + **Shadow thought**: 'I'm not good enough to succeed in this project. I'm not going to take part.'

- **Feeling**: Inadequacy, rejection.

- **Belief**: 'I will fail.'

This can take some time, so be gentle with yourself as it requires you to face your own reflection and allow yourself to be in the feeling. With this part of the practice, it's important to note that there's nothing that needs to change here, you're merely acknowledging your feelings and observing your inner dialogue. Call on the Violet Flame to hold you as you work through this part of the practice.

3. Once you've identified your thoughts and observed how they make you feel, to ensure you don't bypass your shadows it's important you bring awareness to their root cause and the underlying reason it exists. What does your shadow need in order to be integrated? How can you address this need with love and compassion?

4. With the shadow thoughts that you've journaled, I invite you now to bring them into the light. Call on the Violet Flame to support you in illuminating the pathway of the shadows so you can see clearly where they began, what they're rooted in and how to bring them into the light. For example:

    - **Shadow thought**: 'I'm not good enough to succeed in this project. I'm not going to take part.'

    - **The root of this shadow**: My fear of failure stems from childhood experiences of criticism and rejection when I gave things a go. (*NB: There may be a specific event that stands out for you, so you can jot this down, too.*)

- **What does my shadow need to bring it into the light?** My shadow needs validation.

- **How can I integrate my shadow?** I need to give myself validation. I will do this by praising myself more when I'm contributing and giving things a go, and I will celebrate myself for showing up.

As the observer, you're now aware of regular shadow thoughts, the underlying patterns and beliefs they've revealed, where the roots come from, and what's needed to integrate the shadows. We can now bring in the true transformation, which is choosing to write a new story and changing the outcome as a result.

5. Now revisit the original shadow thought, and with loving intention, rewrite the unkind statement into a kinder, more supportive narrative. Acknowledge the shadow aspect without judgment but choose to empower yourself with a new perspective rooted in love, abundance, and self-compassion. For example:

    - **Shadow thought**: 'I'm not good enough to succeed in this project. So, I'm not going to take part.'

    - **New story**: 'I am capable of success in this project, and I deserve to take part.'

    - **New feeling**: Confidence and self-worth.

    - **New belief**: 'I've already succeeded in this project regardless of the outcome purely because I've been part of it.'

6. As you rewrite your narrative, use the Violet Flame. Visualize it burning through those shadows. As it begins to light you up, it is transforming the shadows into new words and thoughts. These

new words bring forward a new frequency – allow yourself to go into the new feeling and see the Violet Flame creating a different belief within your subconscious. See this belief imprinting new patterns and opening up new timelines for your life.

7. As you engage in this practice of choosing change, observe how your days begin to shift in response to your conscious choices. Notice the subtle transformations in your mood, energy, and perception of reality as you transmute shadows into light. Trust in the power of the Violet Flame as it guides and supports you. Remember, with each thought, each choice, you shape the reality you experience.

You can revisit this practice as much as you require. Over time, this will become a natural part of your processing. And the more you become aware, the quicker the realizations. Then transformation will happen, meaning that the practice is sped up. You won't need to write things down because you know yourself so well you can transform those shadows before they even get a chance to finish their sentence! You'll get to a point where you're able to see your life as a tapestry; the thoughts are the threads, and you can be in flow with creating the bigger picture for the life that you wish to experience.

CHAPTER 4

Forgiveness Flame

'This flame does not hold grudges,'
the Violet Flame burned softly.
'And neither must you.'

'How can I forgive?' I asked, my voice trembling.
'The pain is still so real. The memory runs so deep.'

The Flame flickered brighter, its warmth filling me.
'Forgiveness is not for them,' it said gently.
'It is for you. It is the key that unlocks the
chains you have bound yourself in.
Forgiveness does not say what happened was right,
it says you are no longer willing to let the past define you.
Let go of the punishment you've carried in your heart,
for it serves only your own suffering.'

A tear slid down my cheek as I whispered,
'Where do I even begin?'

'Begin with willingness,' the Violet Flame answered.
'Willingness to put resentment to rest.
Willingness to hold the younger version of
yourself with love instead of blame.
Willingness to see where the light has dimmed in others.
It doesn't excuse their actions; however,
it can bring you to the understanding:
Every soul is doing their best with what they have.'

I knew then, I was not meant to carry the weight of my
lessons forever. I closed my eyes and imagined it all,
the people, the pain, the echoes of regret,
I offered it to the fire. The Violet Flame transmuted it all;
from this fuel the fire burned brighter.
And I felt lighter.

Forgiveness frees us from cycles of pain and blame as we drop into our hearts, feeling rather than thinking, and are able to have compassion for what is and has been. Naturally, when you welcome the Violet Flame into your life, you're also inviting the force of forgiveness. Forgiveness is choosing peace through the merging of mind and heart, as union is the way of the Violet Flame.

Pathway to Peace

To forgive is commonly thought of as a deeply emotional experience, as indeed it stirs up feelings within. However, it also operates powerfully within the realms of the mind, where we often hold on to stories and judgments that keep us frozen in time. It's the mind that yearns for certainty, constantly seeking external explanations, justifications, and a place to assign blame. When we bring in the Violet Flame of forgiveness, it burns through this type of mental rigidity – it clears the threads that lead us to thinking we need to know 'why,' and instead we open the heart to love; a love that accepts life, and ourselves, as we are.

When we bring in forgiveness through connecting with the Violet Flame, we no longer cling to the need for answers or trawl through our mind attempting to bring rationale to a situation.

We let go of that 'I need to know' mental space that can keep us endlessly looping a scenario or person in our minds. When we forgive, we transmute the need to assign fault and, instead, we surrender our search for explanation. Any urges we had to perpetuate drama or hold on to the past can be dissipated.

By consciously working with the Violet Flame, you step into an empowered state – where forgiveness becomes active transformation of the Self, a courageous declaration that you choose love over fear, and peace over turmoil.

Forgiveness, in truth, has multiple layers or bandwidths. It begins with self-compassion, acknowledging our own humanity, accepting ourselves, and becoming aware of the harsh judgments we carry, so they can be neutralized. As we cultivate self-forgiveness, we increase our capacity to expand this compassion outward, forgiving others, and healing relationships. This enables us to move forward, and through rewriting past stories we can experience great shifts in our lives.

When forgiveness ripples through the entirety of the collective, we can achieve peace on earth.

Yeshua and Mary Magdalene are the Keepers of the Flame who we can call on to guide us through forgiveness. Many believe that their ability to forgive so deeply allowed them to transcend ordinary limitations, so they could perform miracles. Forgiveness opens the heart and spirit, creating inner peace and compassion where pure divine energy can flow freely through the human body. This is how miracles take place; from the expression of a heart that has no conditions or limitations. A heart that fully receives divinity in its entirety is then capable of creating beyond bounds, therefore manifesting things that could be perceived to others as complete miracles.

At the furthest end of the forgiveness spectrum, we can essentially reach a collective state of unconditional, universal love that could merge us fully back to oneness, where this physical world of separation would cease to exist.

> 'When all is forgiven, forgiveness itself no longer exists, and we are left with only truth. True forgiveness is merciless because it returns everything to its source and is a force of pure annihilation. The ultimate goal of forgiveness is in fact to bring an end to the world of form itself.'
> RICHARD RUDD, *THE GENE KEYS*

Personal Renewal

Self-forgiveness is a practice that requires gentleness and can sometimes feel delicate to navigate as it means being totally honest with yourself. Honesty is the starting line, as a big part of self-forgiveness is first becoming aware of your inner realms and bringing awareness to where you're carrying both expressed or repressed feelings of guilt and shame.

When you connect to the Violet Flame for support in transforming these aspects, the past no longer weighs you down and you can come into the truth of who you are beyond your perceived past 'errors.' Self-forgiveness not only supports you in letting go of isolated mistakes; it's transforming the very threads of your suffering, freeing you from the emotional chains or pain within the body that have been created through self-judgment, criticism, self-imposed conditions, or limiting beliefs. In self-forgiveness, you can rewrite stories of the past through the eyes of compassion and clear the way for greater self-love.

First, we must begin self-forgiveness by giving ourselves grace. Remember, we live in a world that's full of judgment and comparison, it's part of this human experience for the ego mind to be critical. So, too, society is shaped by a set of laws that govern us from birth, and we're taught very early on in life that there's a right and wrong. Naturally, placing judgment on ourselves and judging others has become normalized. By connecting with the Violet Flame to bring forgiveness, we choose to alchemize denser energy and focus on creating a different outcome.

To call on the Violet Flame for self-forgiveness, you must do the following three things:

Allow

To allow something is to be spacious. By allowing things to be as they are, for allowing ourselves to be as we are, is the very act of turning within and is representative of the body. The process of allowing has the purpose to open us up from the inside out, and when it comes to forgiveness, it's acknowledging any pain within the body or feelings of suffering, and simply allowing them to be. Allowing yourself to be with the pain. Sometimes, when we begin to revisit painful situations or experiences, we might have a tendency to disembody or distract ourselves, to avoid being with the pain or emotions. However, to forgive, we must first allow, and that means staying with the body.

As in Chapter 3, where we observed our thoughts, here, within the Forgiveness Flame, we observe the feelings. Once we've allowed space for the feelings, we can bring in acceptance.

Accept

Acceptance is all about taking the slow and soft approach to life, which is also the path of grace. It's important to remember that the Violet Flame, although a powerful force, is both the roaring flames and the glowing embers. It takes strength to be soft. This softening process of accepting without judgment builds momentum with forgiveness as it brings a new awareness and energy.

Acceptance is what can then follow as a result of being with the feeling. When we've given space to acknowledge, and be in touch with, how we feel through allowing it all to be, acceptance happens as we remember our heart. Remembering that we are OK, we begin to trust again that we'll always be OK. With acceptance, there's always hope of life. Life itself is hope, and as already mentioned in Chapter 3, hope is one of the places you find the Violet Flame burning bright.

Divine grace is the treasure to be uncovered on this earthly journey. Acceptance is the map which leads us to this bounty. When we accept everything as it is in our lives right now, when we accept ourselves as we are right now, we have embraced life. The more you accept yourself, allow yourself and life to be as it is, the less constriction presents itself, and instead, expansion arises. Meaning new opportunities and experiences will flow in because there's space for them.

Embrace

To embrace is when the mind can come in. Embracing is to realize within our awareness that creation wants to be experienced through us. When we embrace this, regardless of what's happened in the past, we continue forward with hope, head held high, open-hearted, receiving the beauty of life. Through the process of self-forgiveness, we allow our souls to finally be free. With the space we've created through allowing and the acceptance that brings us out from suffering, we can embrace what's here for us and we can let the fullness of life in.

Allowing is in the body, embrace is in the mind, and acceptance is the bridge that brings them into union. This is the Violet Flame of forgiveness doing its work. As Richard Rudd also shares in *The Gene Keys*, allowing, accepting, and embracing are universal principles of forgiveness, found in every path of grace.

Can you allow yourself to be, can you accept yourself fully, embrace all of creation, and what is being experienced through you?

Yes, courageous soul, with the Violet Flame, you can.

Practicing Self-Forgiveness

This practice is for you to explore the areas where you require forgiveness to yourself. It will help you transform any threads of shame, self-judgment, and guilt that you're either consciously aware of or subconsciously suppressing. You'll confront the places within yourself that hold suffering or pain, allowing the space so they can be acknowledged, accepted, and embraced through softening, gentleness, compassion, and grace.

You'll also call on the support of Yeshua and Mary Magdalene, Keepers of the Violet Flame and our greatest teachers of forgiveness.

1. As we've done in the previous chapters, prepare yourself a space where you won't be distracted. You may choose to light a violet candle or hold a piece of amethyst as a physical representation of the Violet Flame. Sit or lie down comfortably, taking a few deep breaths to center yourself and make sure you feel anchored and grounded before starting the practice.

2. Prepare yourself a playlist (or play an album) that you can put on to assist you throughout. Choose any soft music you like, which you can move to gently and that brings you feelings of peace. Remember, if any sensations or emotions become too intense for you during this practice, gently come back to stillness and refocus on your breath using that as your anchor back to the present moment.

3. Sit comfortably and close your eyes. Bring your awareness into your body and your natural breath. Allow yourself to come into presence with the sensation of being in a physical form. How does

your body feel? Feel the weight of it on the ground, focus on your senses. What can you hear? How does your skin feel? Gently, open the eyes slightly. What can you see? How does the air smell?

4. When you feel ready to do so, begin to introduce some gentle movement. Focus on your body and start to stretch, moving up from the feet, scanning each part of your body right up to your head, taking your time so you can really be present with each area. As you go through scanning and stretching each part of your body, gently notice where you feel tension and heaviness. These sensations might represent emotions or pain that you've been holding for a long time. At this point we're allowing these sensations merely to be acknowledged, just as they are. Remember, they are sensations within the body; try not to attach anything to them, merely observing.

5. Silently or aloud, say:

> 'I call upon the Violet Flame, the transformative light of forgiveness, to envelop me now. I invite Yeshua and Mary Magdalene, Keepers of this Flame, to be with me in this sacred space, guiding me through my process of self-forgiveness.'

6. Gently invite in some space for self-enquiry by asking yourself:

    + What past actions, thoughts, or experiences bring me feelings of shame, guilt, or regret?
    + Where do I judge myself?
    + Where do I create or perpetuate drama in my life?

    Trust whatever comes up and allow yourself to feel these emotions fully. There's no need to rush; be present with each feeling, knowing you're held within the Violet Flame's light.

7. As you observe these feelings and sensations in the body, remind yourself to approach them with neutrality. You're not here to analyze or rush to fix anything – only to allow whatever needs to be felt to come to the surface. Repeat to yourself:

> 'I allow myself to feel all parts of me. I allow myself to be present with these feelings and sensations, knowing that they are part of the whole. I allow myself space to be with what is.'

> Affirm: 'I am here.'

8. Take a few deep breaths, bringing a sense of calm and softness into your heart. Feel the presence of Yeshua and Mary Magdalene, reminding you of the loving grace you're worthy of. Imagine the Violet Flame glowing softly around your heart, feel your heart beating. The heart is more than just emotions – it's where the soul speaks. Feel the purity of your heart, which comes without conditions.

9. Remind yourself that to feel shame, guilt, or regret is part of the human experience. These feelings are neither right nor wrong; they simply reflect aspects of the journey you've walked and the experiences you've encountered. Repeat to yourself:

> 'I accept myself as I am. I honor the experiences I've been through, knowing they have brought me to this moment of self-forgiveness.'

10. As you stay connected to your heart, allow any lingering thoughts of blame or judgment to fade away. With the Violet Flame's presence, gently begin to visualize these stories burning away gently, leaving space for self-acceptance.

What is it you've always wanted to hear? Say these words to yourself now. For example:

- 'I am human, and I am learning. I embrace the wisdom I've gained from my past.'

- 'I honor my journey, including the challenges. I am worthy of love and compassion.'

- 'I forgive myself fully, knowing that I have always done the best I could with the awareness I had.'

- 'I transform threads of self-judgment, and instead, I choose to see myself through the eyes of love and understanding. I forgive myself fully.'

- 'Creation is experiencing itself through me – every experience has shaped me and brought me closer to knowing my true self.'

11. Envision the Violet Flame expanding outward from your heart, filling every part of your being. Feel this energy of forgiveness dissolving old constrictions and constraints within your emotional and physical body, creating a vast, open space within you. This space represents the new opportunities, freedom, and inner peace that you're inviting in.

12. Bring an image to mind of yourself standing strong, and if you wish, stand strong in your physical body, too. See yourself standing with an open heart and lifted gaze, embracing life's beauty. This is your empowered self, walking forward without the chains of past judgments, shame, or guilt. Feeling free in your body, know that with the Violet Flame, you will live each day with grace and resilience. Repeat to yourself:

> *'I embrace all that I am, all that I have been, and all that I will be. I choose hope, peace, and compassion as I open my heart fully to life.'*

13. Take a few moments in silence, sensing the gentle but profound shifts within you as you allowed space, came into acceptance, and then embraced yourself fully. Allow yourself to feel the peace, love, and openness that emerge from self-forgiveness. Feel the glowing embers of the Violet Flame warming you within. Feel the space created within the body, as the sensations no longer bring discomfort or pain. Feel the heart expanded with greater capacity for compassion.

14. Place both hands over your heart and bow your head slightly in gratitude. Thank yourself for your courage in facing these feelings, allowing them to be acknowledged, and for your willingness to transform them through acceptance. Thank Yeshua and Mary Magdalene for guiding you through this process, reminding you that they are always with you when you call upon them.

15. If you lit a candle, gently blow it out, symbolizing the completion and closing of this practice. Know that the Violet Flame still burns within you, carrying forward the forgiveness and grace you've cultivated.

16. Slowly open your eyes and take a few deep breaths. Feel the weight of your body supported by the ground, and take a few moments to adjust, re-entering the present with a renewed sense of peace and clarity.

By integrating this practice into your life as often as you feel you need, you continue the journey of self-forgiveness, opening space within to embrace all that life has to offer. Let the Violet Flame guide you whenever you feel that you need to allow space to acknowledge, accept, and embrace yourself. Each time you practice, you deepen your relationship with yourself, and you increase your capacity to experience peace within.

✦

Relationship Revamp

The Violet Flame also assists us in extending the energy of forgiveness to the outer world, exploring where in our lives we can bring compassion to others. As we work through our personal histories and embrace this concept, we realize a deep truth: Nothing is ever truly personal. However, this is where a paradox plays out, because although nothing is ever personal, everyone around us acts as a mirror. When we begin to embody the energy of the Violet Flame, we see more clearly the aspects of ourselves that are being shown via their reflection.

When we forgive someone, we're not saying we agree with the way in which they behaved or the choices they made, nor are we looking to affirm what was right vs what was wrong. However, just as we did with self-forgiveness, we are allowing and accepting a person or situation to be, so we can embrace life, and move forward feeling liberated and empowered. Through forgiveness, we're unravelling the knots of resentment and guilt that we may have been harboring within, and instead, we're giving way to a profound sense of freedom.

One of the most significant relationships I was able to heal in my life through the Violet Flame of forgiveness was the one with my dad. The relationship had always been a complex one. My mum and dad divorced when I was around five years old. My memories of us all living together in our first home are faint and most of what I remember of my dad came after the split – my mum had custody, so we only spent every other weekend together.

My dad was often described as a 'lovable nightmare.' He was the quintessential 'boy about town' – fast-living, fast-talking, and utterly ruled by his addictive personality. Alcohol, smoking, gambling, women. I observed his life as a constant chase for the next thrill. Quite the 'Del Boy,' he was a wheeler-dealer. His worth was wrapped in material things: designer clothes, flashy cars, and a big house.

His main form of communication? Banter. Relentlessly poking fun was his love language. Yet try explaining that to an eight-year-old child. I didn't hear love through his jokes; I often heard criticism. I took it all literally, internalizing it, and it chipped away at my self-esteem.

He was the life of the party – the guy everyone wanted to know, the man who went straight to the front of the queue at the club, a blonde on his arm, and buying drinks for everyone at the bar. People adored him because he was fun, unpredictable, the life and soul of a gathering.

As a child, I just wanted my dad to be *my dad*. I couldn't understand why he'd rather spend Christmas Eve out in town drinking than being with his family. Watching him stumble through the door on Christmas morning, only to spend the rest of the day passed out in bed while I sat with his girlfriend downstairs – those memories remain always. My stepmum cared for me and my sister in ways I'll always appreciate, but she could never replace the presence and acknowledgment I so deeply craved from my dad.

When I reached my early twenties, my dad and stepmum separated. She moved out of their big house, and I moved in with him. He prepared a bedroom for me – painted it, bought me furniture. I remember feeling elated. Finally, I thought, my dad was making space for me in his life!

That time was chaotic – a blur of late nights and lost days. My dad's house turned into a party house, and I did pretty much whatever I wanted. We began to bond, finding common ground in going out drinking and clubbing.

One explosive argument shattered everything. I don't even remember the details anymore, only the aftermath. My dad threw me out of the house, making me homeless in an instant. The bond we'd been building crumbled, and a year later, he moved to Thailand. For the next 14 years, we hardly spoke.

In 2023, something shifted within me. I felt a deep, undeniable calling to see my dad. The pull was so strong I couldn't ignore it. At first, I had no idea how to make it happen – logistically, financially, emotionally. But I knew the first step: I needed to reach out.

I found him on Facebook and sent him a message. Within hours, we were on the phone. We talked for four hours, catching up on 14 years of mainly silence. Something was different. I could see my dad clearly, not through the lens of my expectation but as a man navigating life in his own imperfect way. We laughed a lot. True to form, he messed with me for being into 'woo-woo' magic. 'So, what's all this magic you're into then?' he teased, but I could tell he was intrigued.

I tried to explain it – spiritual concepts, the ways creation works, my understanding of life. To my surprise, he listened. I noticed how much I was like him: free-thinking, creative, adventurous. I'd spent so many years focusing on what he hadn't provided me, that I never noticed the gifts he *had* passed down.

At the end of the call, I told him, 'I'm coming to see you. Will you be there to meet me?'

He paused. 'I'm going to be honest with you,' he said. 'I'm on my arse. I've spent six months on the sofa doing nothing. I've lost my mojo. I don't know what to do anymore.'

'I don't need you to give me anything, Dad,' I replied. 'I just want some of your time. Your presence.'

'Done,' he said.

It all manifested faster than I could have imagined. Within days, I had time off work, the money I needed, and someone to care for my cats. I booked my flight. That evening, I sat with the Violet Flame, knowing this journey was about far more than seeing my dad.

I called on the Violet Flame to help me release the pain I'd carried for so long. The belief that I was unlovable, born from years of feeling invisible to him. The anxious attachment that left me terrified of abandonment, playing out again and again in my adult relationships. The hyper-independence that drove me to exhaustion because I never trusted anyone to show up for me.

I cried as I let the Violet Flame cocoon me in its violet light. I felt it soothing me, transmuting the pain into something lighter. I accepted everything – the absence, the chaos, the heartbreak – and I embraced the beauty within it. I saw the ways it shaped me, the lessons it taught me, and the ways I'd grown because of it.

Most importantly, I knew I couldn't go to Thailand seeking an apology or trying to be heard. That energy would only keep the old stories alive. I knew from our phone conversation, my dad already carried shame for the father he hadn't been. I didn't need to add to it. I just needed to go and love him. Unconditionally. To see him as he was – not through labels or expectations, but as a man doing his best with the tools he'd been given. I imagined him sitting in front of me. I dropped into my heart and said, 'Dad, I love you unconditionally. I accept all of you, as you are.' The Violet Flame expanded within me, burning away the past. For the first time in my life, I looked at myself and said, 'I AM lovable,' and I truly believed it.

Two days later, my phone rang. 'You're not going to *believe* this,' my dad said, almost breathless.

He told me a lawyer had contacted him out of the blue. He'd forgotten about three small plots of land he'd bought 14 years ago in Georgia, USA, and now a property developer wanted to buy them. 'Can you believe it? This means I can live out the rest of my days here in Thailand like a king! Maybe there's something to this magic you talk about!'

At the end of the call, he said three words to me for the first time, which rippled through every cell in my body: 'I love you.'

When I arrived at Bangkok airport, part of me wondered if he'd show up, my inner child was nervous. I looked up and there he was, coming down the escalator with a spring in his step, instantly making fun of my 'rainbow hippie' outfit.

During that visit, my dad showed up for me in ways I'd always dreamed of. He gave me his time, his presence, and his care. He provided for me entirely. He arranged incredible experiences, introduced me to everyone he knew, and proudly told anyone who'd listen, 'This is my daughter!' I could see it in his face: He was so happy I was there. We played pool together at his club, he won the championship, and people were stopping to shake his hand and call him 'the Champion.' He felt like 'the man' and his mojo was back.

We had the best time and it was as if the entirety of our relationship had been rewritten.

It was through the Forgiveness Flame that the energetics shifted between my dad and I, and as a result, we both got to rewrite the past so we could experience a new reality.

Forgiving Others

This exercise will assist you in healing the relationships in your life and freeing yourself from the stories of the past.

1. As we've done in previous practices, prepare your space, then ground and center yourself. Set an intention around who you're

bringing forgiveness to – it can be more than one person at a time; you can call in multiple people if you wish to.

2. Begin by bringing the Violet Flame into your awareness. In the previous practices we've called the Violet Flame forward using various techniques, so connect with it in a way that resonates with you (through an invocation, visualization, tools etc.).

3. Light a candle and allow yourself to feel any emotions or memories that surface as you reflect on the person or relationship you're healing. Notice any beliefs or attachments you hold, whether from childhood or later experiences, that have shaped you. Allow any emotions, such as anger, sadness, grief, to come to the surface without judgment. This is the time to acknowledge all your feelings openly. (*A reminder: As with other practices, if anything becomes too intense, take a pause. Use your own discernment around what feels best for you.*)

4. Gently bring your focus to all aspects of the relationship. Accept the journey you've had with this person, including both the challenges and the gifts it brought to your life. Reflect on any qualities or positive aspects you've inherited or learned through this relationship. Acknowledge any urges you may have to make the person see things differently. Remember, forgiveness is not needing to control, and accepting things as they are. This is about *your* process, rather than trying to change *them*. Trust that the Violet Flame will guide you, without your need to force anything.

5. Imagine the person, people, or situation you wish to transform through forgiveness standing before you, free from any roles, expectations, conditions, or labels. See them simply as a human being, with their own challenges and journey. Allow them to exist in this space with you, held by the presence of the Violet Flame's

gentle light, while you look through the lens of compassion. Acknowledge that they're doing the best they can within their own life path.

6. Now tune in to the love within your own heart, as vast and infinite as you can imagine. Let this love expand outward, flowing toward the person or people you're forgiving. Say silently or aloud:

    'I love you, I see you. I fully accept you as you are.'

7. Feel the Violet Flame assisting you, gently dissolving old resentments or judgments. Turn your attention inward, affirming your own worth. Affirm a new pathway that will transform old patterns this relationship may have fostered in the past. Here, you fully embrace compassion.

8. When you feel ready, gently blow out the candle, symbolizing the end of the ritual. Open your eyes and feel the peaceful liberation this practice has brought, knowing that forgiveness has set you free. This practice may need to be revisited on several occasions as forgiveness can take time, it can be a process, and be gentle with yourself if you need more time.

Remember, the power of the Violet Flame can transform your past stories, your relationships and, as a result, it will change the manifested physical reality you get to experience. Be aware of things that begin to change and evolve from carrying out this practice. You may like to keep a journal so you can record the ways in which your life begins to move.

CHAPTER 5

Unified Flame

'There is a holy dance within you,' the Violet Flame flickered.
'It is a sacred rhythm where masculine and
feminine energies move together in harmony,
and where the inner child plays freely. To learn
the moves of this dance, you have to listen.'

I closed my eyes, breathing in the warmth of the Flame.
'They all speak so differently,' I replied.
'The masculine demands action, structure, and clarity.
The feminine yearns for flow, softness, and surrender.
And the child... the child just wants to feel safe and loved.
How do I bridge their voices?'

The Violet Flame flickered brighter, its essence expanding.
'You must become your own sanctuary,' it said,
as purple fractals swirled out from the fire.
'A sacred space where each part feels seen,
heard, and honored.'

I felt the pull of my heart as the truth of
these words settled deep within me.
'How do I create this?' I asked.

The Flame crackled gently, its violet hue shimmering.
'Through love,' it said simply. 'Love is the bridge.
Sit with each aspect, listen to their needs,
honor their wisdom. Once they feel heard,
invite them into harmony. Call upon my light to
weave their energies together in unity. Then let them
dance together in the sacred space of your heart.'

I placed my hand on my chest, feeling the warmth
of the Violet Flame radiate within me.

'You are the holy trinity,' the Flame continued.
'You are the mother, the father, and the child.
As the unified flame, your spirit is whole,'
the Violet Flame whispered, its light becoming softer.
'You are already complete. Now, remember the dance.'

And as the Flame's glow settled into my heart, I realized:
When the masculine is of service to the feminine and
the feminine is of devotion to the masculine,
together they create a perfect home for the child.
The union I longed for was not somewhere outside me,
a whole family unit was already inside me.

Creation, Creator, God, Divine Beloved, Source is the whole, it is us, and it is all. The Violet Flame burns through the shadows and brings forth the light, so we can find our truth and experience the love that we are. The essence of our wholeness lies in these internal energies: the masculine, the feminine, and the inner child. Together, they form a holy trinity.

When we begin to recognize how these energies express themselves in both their shadow and divine aspects, we gain a deeper understanding of what can assist us in navigating and nurturing our internal world to thrive. Yet, in a society that emphasizes external validation and encourages us to seek resources outside ourselves, our inner flame can either become extinguished, or on the other end of the spectrum, burn out.

When we neglect our holy trinity, fragmentation can occur. Over time, we may feel disconnected, and unknowing of how to truly listen within. The Violet Flame can be a constant source of light when tended to. This light will illuminate our path back to ourselves and help us reclaim our wholeness.

Inner Union

A divine dance lies within each of us – a delicate interplay of masculine and feminine energies that transcends gender or identity. These two energies are the foundational principles of creation. The masculine energy provides structure, the container in which the feminine energy flows and creates. Without structure, the feminine's creative potential would have no form; without the feminine's vitality and inspiration, the masculine would remain motionless.

This synergy is reflected in everything, from the birthing of stars in the cosmos to the blooming of flowers on Earth. It's a relationship of profound interdependence, where neither energy can exist in isolation nor fulfill its purpose without the other.

Mary Magdalene and Yeshua are the Keepers of the Flame who can support the inner union of our masculine and feminine energies. When these ascended masters walked the Earth, Magdalene was an embodiment of the divine feminine, while Yeshua was the embodiment of the divine masculine. Their sacred union serves as a blueprint for harmonizing these energies within.

The Feminine Principle

Feminine energy is the flowing stream of intuition, creativity, nurture, and receptivity. It's the wisdom of surrender, the ability to feel deeply, and the sparks of inspiration that breathe life into all things. It's the stillness, the deep listening, and the oracle that guides.

Our relationship with our mother, or a maternal figure, often influences how this energy develops. If the mother cultivated emotional connection, encouraged vulnerability, and modeled self-love, the inner feminine flourishes. Conversely, if the mother was overly critical, unavailable, or smothering, this can create inversions within the inner feminine.

Balanced/divine feminine expression:

- Emotional intelligence and the ability to feel deeply

- Trust in intuition and inner guidance

- Creativity, flow, expression, and surrender to the unknown

- Self-compassion and the ability to nurture oneself and others

- Receptivity – openness to love, abundance, and support

Shadow/distorted feminine expression:

- Emotional overwhelm or difficulty regulating emotions

- Creating chaos, perpetuating drama, and manipulating

- People-pleasing or self-sacrifice

- Hyper-independence, not allowing any support

- Suppression of intuition and difficulty trusting the Self or others

- A tendency to over-give while neglecting and abandoning personal needs

The Masculine Principle

Masculine energy represents action, focus, stability, and the structure that provides direction in our lives. It's the steady rhythm of forward momentum, the ability to take decisive steps, and the protector and container that creates safe spaces for growth. It's the motivation, determination, and force within us that leads.

Our relationship with our father, or a father figure, often plays a significant role in how this energy is expressed. If the father provided a consistent sense of safety, encouragement, and presence, the inner masculine is likely to manifest as confident leadership, healthy boundaries, and a strong sense of direction. However, if the father was absent, overly critical, or emotionally distant, this can create inversions in how the masculine energy is expressed.

Balanced/divine masculine expression:

- Confidence in taking action and leading with clarity
- The ability to set and maintain healthy boundaries
- A strong sense of direction and purpose
- Stability, reliability, and the capacity to protect and provide
- Logical thinking without dismissing intuition

Shadow/distorted masculine expression:

- Overworking, striving, always trying to 'fix,' and proving worth through achievement

- Controlling, rigid, and being 'right'
- Suppression of emotions and a tendency to bypass vulnerability
- Reactive outbursts of anger when presented with triggers
- Harsh inner criticism or judgment of Self and others
- Avoidance, withdrawal, or fear of responsibility

✦

When all these energies are equally honored, they create a sacred union within us. Yet, in today's world, this balance has been disrupted. We live in a patriarchal society that's long exalted the masculine principle, while suppressing the feminine. The emphasis on productivity, logic, and achievement – while valuable – has overshadowed the equally vital qualities of rest, intuition, and emotional depth. This imbalance has not only shaped the world around us but also created discord within our inner worlds.

The suppression of feminine energy is nothing new – it's been part of history for centuries. Religious teachings have often favored hierarchy and control, placing masculine principles at the forefront, while silencing the wisdom and power of the feminine. One of the most profound examples of feminine suppression can be found during the witch trials. Women and men who carried the feminine principles of healing and intuition, who had a connection to nature and the plant kingdoms, were tried, persecuted, and killed.

The witch hunters pushed individuals into betraying their neighbors, acquaintances, friends, and family members, forcing them to make accusations in a desperate attempt to protect themselves from being targeted. This era literally programmed people to turn on the feminine, it created division and imprinted fear within our DNA. Not only in women but throughout humanity, as it stripped society of its feminine essence.

The consequence of this suppression has left its mark on all of us, regardless of gender. It's created a world where we often over-identify with the masculine traits of doing and achieving, while neglecting the feminine qualities of being and receiving. This disconnection manifests as burnout, discontent, and a deep sense of incompleteness.

The way our inner masculine and feminine energies are expressed is profoundly shaped by the relationship we have with our parents or primary caregivers. These initial bonds act as a blueprint for how we embody these energies, impacting how we relate to ourselves, others, and the world around us. Over time, the imprints left by these relationships can ripple into adulthood, influencing our behaviors, choices, and emotional responses as these early dynamics created a framework for our interaction with the world.

Yet, these imprints are not unchangeable. Through conscious awareness and calling on the Violet Flame, we can transmute inherited distortions and embody the divine expression of our inner masculine and feminine energies. The Violet Flame merges these principles, transcending duality to bring them into harmony by illuminating them with all-encompassing love and neutrality. With this illumination, we begin to better tend to our needs so we can come into balance and integrate all aspects of this divine union.

An integrated inner feminine encourages us to:

- Embrace our emotions and feel without fear.

- Trust our intuition, use our voice, and honor our inner wisdom.

- Create from a place of inspiration rather than from panic or lack.

- Have the courage to surrender to the flow of life.

An integrated inner masculine enables us to:

- Take action with purpose and clarity.

- Set healthy boundaries and stand in self-sovereignty.

- Provide stability and a strong foundation for ourselves and others.

- Lead with confidence, rather than from fear or control.

Together, they create a powerful synergy. The masculine provides the structure in which the feminine can flow freely, and the feminine breathes life and inspiration into the masculine's framework.

As the Violet Flame burns away distortions, we begin to see the divine essence of our inner masculine and feminine, allowing them to coexist in harmony. Within this shift, we also begin to prioritize self-care over self-sacrifice. We honor the masculine's need for structure, while also embracing the feminine's call to flow. We create a balance where we can think logically without losing touch with our intuition. We take time out to nurture ourselves, without losing sight of our goals. We start to place as much emphasis on rest and stillness as we do on forward movement and action.

The Violet Flame reminds us that we're not separate from the dance of creation – we are the dance itself. In this state of inner union, we no longer look to the external world to complete us. We no longer seek validation or approval from others, because we've found the love, strength, and wisdom within ourselves. We become the embodiment of union.

Coming into Inner Union

This ritual invites you to acknowledge, honor, and harmonize your inner masculine and feminine energies, bringing them into divine union through the illumination of the Violet Flame.

1. To begin, make sure you're sitting comfortably, then place both hands, palms up, on your thighs. Each hand represents an essential aspect of your being:

    + Your right hand symbolizes your inner masculine energy – the courage, action, focus, stability, logic, and protector within you. This is where you may also like to visualize and connect with the energy of Yeshua.

    + Your left hand symbolizes your inner feminine energy – the intuition, creativity, vulnerability, nurture, emotion, and surrender that reside within. This is where you may like to visualize and connect with the energy of Mary Magdalene.

2. As you sit with both hands open, acknowledge these energies within you. Affirm:

   'I am both. I am powerful and gentle. I am courageous and vulnerable. I am soft and strong.'

3. Lift your right hand, palm up, and place it over your heart. Visualize the Violet Flame surrounding this hand, clearing shadows such as rigidity, control, or fear of vulnerability. Feel these dense energies dissolving in the Flame, transforming them into strength, clarity, and purpose.

4. Bring your left hand (your feminine energy) to the center and place it gently on top of your right hand at your heart. Allow your feminine energy to hold and nurture your masculine energy. Take a few breaths and express love to this part of yourself through the voice of the feminine:

   'Thank you for your structure, focus, and leadership. I honor the sacred masculine's role in my life. I embrace your divine qualities, and I am in devotion to you.'

5. When you feel ready, place both hands back on your thighs.

6. Now lift your left hand, palm up, and place it over your heart. Visualize the Violet Flame surrounding it, transmuting shadows such as manipulation, unworthiness, or emotional chaos. Feel these denser energies transforming into creativity, intuition, and love.

7. Bring your right hand (your masculine energy) to the center and place it on top of your left hand at your heart. Allow your

masculine energy to hold and support your feminine energy. Take a few breaths and express love to this part of yourself through the voice of the masculine:

> 'Thank you for your intuitive guidance, creativity, and capacity for love. I honor the sacred feminine's role in my life. I embrace your divine qualities, and I am in service to you.'

8. When you feel ready, place both hands back on your thighs.

9. Bring both hands back to your heart center. Visualize the Violet Flame within your heart, see your inner masculine and feminine dancing together here in unison. Feel the warmth of the Violet Flame as it lights you up. Affirm:

> 'I honor and integrate both my masculine and feminine energies. Together, they create sanctity and through this union, I live in divine harmony.'

10. You can stay here for as long as you feel compelled to do so. You can hold the vision of your masculine and feminine energy bathing in violet light as they exquisitely dance together. Observe how beautiful this union is. You may also like to introduce some gentle movement to your physical body. Feel held by the masculine and allow yourself to flow intuitively with the feminine.

11. When your practice feels complete, you can come back to a place of stillness and, with gratitude in your heart, know that this union is within you always, as is the Violet Flame, so you're always surrounded and encompassed by love.

+ ✦ +

Inner Child

Within each of us exists the inner child – a tender aspect of our being that carries the purity, wonder, and joy we were born with. This part of us is timeless, untouched by external labels, full of innocence, imagination, and play. The inner child is the source of our capacity for fun, curiosity, and awe; it holds the keys to our authentic, purest expression.

However, the complexities of adult life can often cause this vital part of us to become forgotten or neglected, buried beneath layers of societal expectations, responsibilities, and over-seriousness.

We're taught to prioritize practicality over play, logic over creativity, and seriousness over joy. With time, this disconnect can distance us from our sense of wonder and spontaneity, leaving the inner child unacknowledged and yearning for attention.

When the inner child is neglected, they don't simply disappear; instead, their unmet needs and unresolved pain manifest unconsciously in our adult lives. The shadow aspects of the inner child can show up as self-doubt, fear of abandonment, perfectionism, or even rebelliousness. These behaviors are often rooted in early experiences where our inner child felt unheard, unseen, or unloved.

The collective shadow of seriousness further exacerbates this disconnection. Society tends to value productivity and achievement over playfulness and joy, perpetuating the belief that 'childish' qualities must be outgrown. This shadow has created a world where many have forgotten how to laugh freely, explore without fear, and create without limitation. The inner child is not a sign of immaturity but rather a source of vitality, inspiration, and freedom.

> *'We don't stop playing because we grow old;*
> *we grow old because we stop playing.'*
> GEORGE BERNARD SHAW

The inner child is the bridge to our deepest joy and creative potential. When we reclaim and honor this part of ourselves, we tap into a reservoir of boundless energy, imagination, and playfulness. The inner child reminds us that life is not solely about responsibilities and goals; it's also about exploration, adventure, and wonder. Our inner child has no agenda or expectation, its heart is pure and through this we can access freedom.

The Violet Flame becomes a powerful ally in connecting to our inner child as it transmutes the shadows of neglect and abandonment, clearing the blocks that prevent us from fully embodying the child's essence. When we call upon the Violet Flame, it lights the way for our natural sense of playfulness and our curiosity to flow freely. It encourages us to explore without fear, embrace our silliness, dance like no one is watching, and enjoy the magic of play – even if it means getting a little messy along the way! Children are often so free in their expression and flow, they live in complete presence, intuitively acting on what they need. Whether that's spinning around in circles, having a meltdown on the floor, only eating oranges for 48 hours, or burying themselves in mud. They look at life through an unfiltered lens.

The Violet Flame helps us see that embracing our inner child is an essential act of self-love. One of the most profound ways to nurture the inner child is through the power of play. Play is a natural expression of our soul. It's in play that we connect to our creative essence, explore new possibilities, and allow ourselves to be fully present in the moment. When we integrate this energy, we realize play is not just an activity or something that can only be experienced during childhood. It's a state of being that also invites us to see the world with fresh eyes.

By transforming the layers of resistance, fear, and control that keep us bound to seriousness, the Violet Flame can help us create space for play. When we allow ourselves to embrace the playful energy of the inner child, we open the door to our limitless self. We become more willing to take risks, try new things, and approach life with a sense of adventure.

To embody the essence of the inner child, consider these practices:

- **Rediscover your hobbies.** Revisit activities that brought you joy as a child, such as painting, dancing, building, or imaginative play.

- **Be curious.** Allow yourself to ask questions, experiment, and explore without needing a specific outcome.

- **Create moments of spontaneity.** Step away from rigid schedules and embrace the freedom to act on inspiration in the moment.

- **Spend time in nature.** The natural world is a playground that invites us to reconnect with our inner child's sense of wonder.

Reconnecting with Your Inner Child

The following practice will guide you to connect with your inner child, understand their needs, and discover ways to bring more play and joy into your life.

1. Find a quiet and comfortable place where you won't be disturbed. Light a candle, close your eyes, and take a few deep breaths. Imagine the Violet Flame surrounding you, creating a loving space for this journey.

2. As you breathe deeply, picture yourself walking into a serene, beautiful meadow bathed in soft violet light. In the center of this meadow, you see your inner child waiting for you. Notice how they look, what they're doing, and how they feel.

3. Approach your inner child with kindness and curiosity. Sit beside them and ask: 'What do you need to feel seen, heard, and loved?' Allow them to express themselves freely. Listen with your heart, offering compassion and understanding.

4. Imagine yourself wrapping your inner child in a warm embrace, assuring them that they are safe, loved, and valued. Invite the Violet Flame to flow through both of you, gently moving through any fear they're holding.

5. Ask your inner child what activities or experiences would bring them joy. It might be playing, creating, exploring, or simply spending time in nature. Make a commitment to your inner child that you'll integrate these elements into your daily life.

6. When you feel ready, thank your inner child and the Violet Flame for this experience. Visualize the meadow gently fading away as you return to the present moment, carrying the essence of your inner child with you.

I encourage you to return to this practice regularly, allowing space for a deep and meaningful connection with your inner child to unfold. At first, they may appear hesitant or guarded, especially if your early experiences in life led to feelings of unease or mistrust. Approach this process with patience, compassion, and self-love, understanding that it may take time for this precious part of you to feel safe enough to emerge fully. If connecting with your inner child stirs emotions or feels overwhelming, use your own discernment and consider seeking additional support to guide you gently on this journey.

As you integrate the energy of the inner child, life becomes more vibrant, more playful, and more meaningful. You reconnect with the magic of simply being alive, becoming less serious, and discovering that the path to wholeness lies in the joyful embrace of the child.

Holy Trinity

The journey to becoming the Unified Flame requires us to nurture and navigate harmony within this inner family unit. When these three aspects of ourselves – the masculine, feminine, and inner child – all move together in balance and unity, we form the holy trinity within. Here, we create that inner sanctuary of love, where structure, intuition, and innocence coexist. Then true transformation occurs, as the synergy of these energies empowers us to navigate life with clarity, creativity, and joy.

The Violet Flame, with its alchemical energy, lights the way in this process, transmuting distortions within the family unit, and illuminating what's needed in each moment. To embody the Unified Flame, we must cultivate deep listening, attuning to the unique voices of our inner family. By calling upon the Violet Flame, we gain clarity on which energy is speaking and how to bring balance, allowing us to self-soothe, self-regulate, and restore inner peace.

Life presents us with countless situations that challenge our sense of equilibrium. When we feel stuck, overwhelmed, or disconnected, it's often because one aspect of our inner family has taken center stage and is struggling on its own. By recognizing which part of the holy trinity is seeking to be heard we can call upon the other members of our inner family to step in and bring the support, guidance, or reassurance that's needed. This is how we master holding space for ourselves.

Here are some examples:

- **The overwhelmed inner child:** You have a million and one tasks to complete, yet you feel frozen and unable to move forward. Your inner child is overwhelmed, whispering, 'I can't do this. It's too much. I want to hide.' This part of you needs the steady grounding of the inner masculine, who steps in to break tasks into manageable steps, create structure, and provide safety through action. Simultaneously, the inner feminine offers emotional reassurance, reminding the inner child that they're supported.

- **The overworked inner masculine:** You've been pushing relentlessly, driven by responsibility and external demands. Exhaustion sets in, leaving you irritable and taking everything extremely seriously. Your inner masculine is overextended. Here, the inner feminine steps in; she encourages a pause, invites rest, and stillness. She brings gentleness and asks you to tend to your emotional needs. Meanwhile, the inner child reminds you to find the cosmic joke, to go out and do something spontaneous to reignite your joy.

- **The suppressed inner feminine:** You've prioritized logic and productivity for so long that you feel uninspired and creatively blocked. Your inner feminine has been suppressed. She needs expression and safe holding. The inner masculine supports by creating the time and space for introspection, while the inner child encourages curiosity and play, helping the feminine return to her natural flow.

When faced with inner turmoil, ask these reflective questions to help identify which part of your holy trinity needs attention:

- What am I feeling right now?
- Which part of my inner family is speaking and seeking regulation?
- What does this part of me need to feel supported and held?
- How can my inner family members show up for me?

This process of harmonizing the holy trinity involves opening up a dynamic dialogue between these three energies. It requires conscious awareness, compassion, and a willingness to honor all aspects of ourselves equally. The Violet Flame acts as a bridge that unites and balances these energies by transmuting any distortions or disharmony. It's the hearth of our inner sanctuary.

In this process of self-regulation and holding, when we call upon the light of the Violet Flame, it alchemizes fear, guilt, and resistance, replacing them with love, neutrality, and clarity. As we symphonize these energies, we begin to recognize their interconnectedness and the moves to this dance are intuitively understood. When we embody the Unified Flame, we no longer move through life feeling fragmented or torn between competing demands. Instead, we approach challenges with a sense of wholeness, knowing that we have the inner resources to meet any situation. We become attuned to our needs and respond to them with clarity and compassion, creating a life that supports our growth and fulfillment.

This state of unity also enhances our relationships with others. When we're in harmony with ourselves, we're better able to communicate, set boundaries, and show up authentically in our connections. We no longer look to others to fill the gaps within us because we've found wholeness within; essentially, through this unity we're completely empowered.

The Violet Flame amplifies this transformation, helping us release old patterns of codependency or self-sacrifice and step into relationships that are rooted in mutual respect, interdependence, and universal love.

Uniting the Holy Trinity

To deepen understanding of your inner family unit and embody the Unified Flame, set aside time for this practice, which honors the masculine, feminine, and inner child within you. The Violet Flame will cleanse and unify these energies.

N.B. You'll need three candles (violet in color or you can use white as an alternative) for lighting during this practice.

As you've done in previous chapters, set your sacred space and ground yourself before you begin (*if you need more guidance on how to prepare, see page 16*).

1. Place your three candles in a triangle. Each one represents an aspect of your inner family unit – masculine (father), feminine (mother) and the inner child.

2. As you light each candle, speak this invocation aloud to awaken the energies of the holy trinity within you and to invite the purifying Violet Flame:

> 'Violet Flame, my sacred light,
> transform my soul, as this family unites;
> Masculine, Feminine and Child divine,
> in harmony now, these aspects align.
> I merge these flames, as one they burn,
> with this harmony, peace returns.
> My holy trinity, strong, soft, and whole,
> this Unified Flame, restores my soul.
> Within this light, I weave a home,

> an inner sanctuary, where I'm never alone.
> Here you dwell, my sacred three,
> in peace, in truth, in unity.'

Take a moment to gaze at the candlelight.

3. Focus on the first candle, symbolizing your inner father. Visualize a steady, strong presence – a guardian and the leader within you. Say:

> 'Inner Masculine, protector bold, what do
> you need for your truth to unfold?'

Listen for any thoughts, emotions, or sensations that arise.

4. Shift your attention to the second candle, representing your inner mother. See her as a nurturing, intuitive energy – a source of love and wisdom. Say:

> 'Inner Feminine, heart so pure, what do
> you need to feel safe and sure?'

Remain open to what she reveals.

5. Finally, focus on the third candle, embodying your inner child. Envision a playful, radiant energy, full of curiosity and wonder. Say:

> 'Inner Child, of joy and play, what do
> you need to feel loved today?'

Allow any emotions or memories to surface, holding space for them with compassion.

6. After reflecting on what each aspect revealed, take time to journal. Then with this awareness, write vows to your holy trinity. These vows are a promise that you'll honor each of these aspects, their needs, and the gifts that they bring. Some examples are below.

My vow to the Masculine:

*'I vow to honor your strength and leadership.
I promise to create space through asserting boundaries
when focus and structure are needed.
I will allow you to protect and take action with confidence.'*

My vow to the Feminine:

*'I vow to listen to your wisdom and intuition.
I promise to nurture myself with love and compassion.
I will create space for you to flow freely and express your truth.'*

My vow to the Inner Child:

*'I vow to celebrate your joy and innocence.
I promise to listen to your dreams and honor your feelings.
I will give you the freedom to play, imagine,
and explore without expectation.'*

Speak these vows aloud to amplify their potency through the vibration of your voice and see the Violet Flame lighting them up.

7. Now, visualize the light of the three candles merging into a single flame. This is the Unified Flame – the sacred integration of the masculine, feminine, and child within you. (*You can repeat the invocation from the start of the practice if you feel inclined to.*)

8. Imagine this Unified Flame burning brightly in your heart; it is the Violet Flame, radiating balance, harmony, and unity. See how each aspect supports and enhances the others:

   - The masculine provides the structure and protection for the feminine and child.
   - The feminine nurtures and inspires the masculine and child.
   - The child brings joy, purity, and play to the masculine and feminine.

   There is no separation.

9. As the Unified Flame burns brighter within, affirm to yourself:

   'I am whole. I am balanced. I am the Unified Flame. Within me, the holy trinity is complete.'

10. Close the practice by giving gratitude to the Violet Flame and your inner family for their guidance and presence. As you blow out the candles, visualize the Unified Flame continuing to burn brightly within your heart.

Embodying the Unified Flame is a lifelong practice of self-awareness and self-love. As you deepen your connection with your inner family, you'll find greater ease and joy in the day-to-day. The inner sanctuary you've cultivated is one of peace and understanding, without a need for perfection. It's where your masculine, feminine, and inner child work together, honoring each other's needs, and creating the foundation of wholeness. Trust that as you nurture this sanctuary, it will support you in navigating life's challenges.

The Violet Flame will continue to be your ally, illuminating the path to wholeness and transmuting anything that stands in the way of your inner harmony. In this state of union, you become a living embodiment of the holy trinity – an expression of love, wisdom, and creative potential in the world.

CHAPTER 6

Glow Up

'Do you know the map of the cosmos?' the Violet Flame
whispered, its violet shimmer drawing me in.
'It is both intricate and effortless, deliberate and wild.
This is the magic of cocreation, where you are both
the dancer and the dance, the artist and the canvas,
the dreamer and the dream.'

I gazed into the Flame, its violet hues
swirling like nebulae in motion.
'How do I create when it feels like so
much is beyond my control?'

The Violet Flame's warmth wrapping me
like the star mother's embrace.
'You are not here to control.
Control is an illusion that binds the spirit.
Courageous soul, instead, you are here to align – to flow
with the synchronistic currents of the universe, to attune
your actions to the rhythm of your purest intentions.
When you do, you experience magic as a natural state.'

I felt a stirring in my heart,
an ancient knowing was awakening.
'I am always "aligning" to something.
How do I know if it's the truth?'

'Trust the signals,' replied the Violet Flame.
'Creation speaks to you in the language of synchronicity.
Nothing happens by chance.
Yes, you are always aligning to something.
However, the Divine leaves subtle breadcrumbs,
guiding you toward the unfolding of your experience here.

When you invoke my light, I magnify these signals,
illuminating your path and clearing fog
that could cloud your vision.
To live with magic as the default
is to notice these whispers of the universe
and to honor them with your actions.'

'What if I misunderstand the signs?
What if I make the wrong move?' I asked.

The Violet Flame softened, its light a gentle reassurance.
'Ah, the paradox,' it said with a smile in its glow.
'Everything matters, yet nothing matters.
You are both the creator of your reality
and the humble witness of a divine plan,
far greater than your mind can comprehend.
In one moment, your intentions shape worlds.
In the next, you surrender to the flow of all that is.
This is the sacred dance of union
and the space where miracles are born.
And when you feel lost or unsure, call upon my fire.
Let my flames burn away confusion,
clearing the space for trust to grow.
I am the alchemy of intention and surrender,
assisting as you step boldly into the unknown.'

I closed my eyes, feeling these words settle into my being.
'So, to live with magic as my default,' I pondered,
'is to cocreate with purpose, without the need to control,
to honor every intention while trusting that the universe
will carry me where I need to go.
Living the paradox of both fate and
free will, without attachment.'

'Yes,' the Violet Flame affirmed, glowing with quiet power.
'Speak your desires into the world and then let go of how
they unfold. Live as though every moment is your last,
and yet don't cling to anything, know that
the Divine orchestrates the masterpiece.
When you walk this paradox,
you will find that magic is not beyond reach,
as the essence of who you are is magic.'

I opened my eyes to a realm of infinite possibilities.
In that moment, I felt the wonder: of being both infinite
and small, the architect of my life, and the passenger
of a divine journey beyond my understanding.
And for the first time, I surrendered to the mystery.

In the hustle and bustle of modern life, the art of presence often slips through our fingers like grains of sand. Moving through our days on autopilot, caught in a whirlwind of distractions, wondering where time has gone. Yet, beneath the noise, there exists a vortex where intention, intuition, and synchronicity meet, where life unfolds in perfect rhythm, and where magic is the default.

The alchemy of presence is the continuation of the Unified Flame. When we bring together intention (mind), intuition (body), and synchronicity (spirit), we activate the holy trinity of creation, as we've talked about in Chapter 5. Here, we're no longer pushing against the current of life, nor are we passively drifting along. Instead, we're attuned to the harmonious flow of the universe, effortlessly cocreating with the unseen forces that guide our path. For when we sync mind, body, spirit, we create a vortex from which miracles can manifest.

Power of Intention

Intentions are the seeds of creation. They guide the unfolding of our lives, aligning us with experiences, opportunities, and pathways that reflect our hearts. One of the most empowering truths about life is this: We're always aligning with something.

Alignment is not something we lose or fall out of; it's an ever-present process. Whether we're aware of it or not, we're constantly aligning ourselves with the thoughts we think, the beliefs we hold, the choices we make, and actions we take.

When we feel 'out of sorts' or as though life is working against us, it's not that we're out of alignment – it's that we're aligning with unconscious patterns, often rooted in our shadows. By becoming conscious of what we're aligning with, it empowers us to shift our alignment toward our heart's desire...

And guess what, courageous soul? You are aligning yourself to the frequency of the Violet Flame; your shadows are illuminated, you have a deeper awareness of Self, you've cultivated inner union, so you can now *consciously* cocreate with the universe and live from a more intentional place! When we bring our shadows into the light of awareness, something miraculous happens.

The energy we once spent avoiding or feeding these aspects becomes available to us again. By clearing the clutter of old stories and past pain, we open up space within ourselves. From this space, we create the awareness needed to choose our path consciously and align to love, rather than fear.

This is where intention becomes a powerful tool. When we set an intention, we're choosing a focal point for our energy, a direction for our alignment. Intentions act as an inner compass and when these intentions have arisen from the heart, they begin aligning us with experiences that reflect the highest timeline of universal love. Living with intention doesn't require grand gestures or drastic changes. In fact, the beauty of intention lies in its simplicity.

What it does take is absolute presence. Presence is the foundation upon which intention rests. Without presence, even the most beautifully crafted intentions will remain unrealized and go unwitnessed. How often do we find ourselves navigating life on autopilot? We wake up, go through our daily routines, and fall asleep, only to repeat the cycle the next day. This waking sleep disconnects us from magic that can only be experienced in the present moment. When we're not present, we cannot truly live intentionally, and life becomes a series of unconscious reactions rather than empowered choices.

Distraction is another factor that can take us out of presence. Components such as alcohol, certain foods, social media, and excessive screen time can pull us out of presence and into unconscious patterns of behavior. These activities aren't inherently 'bad,' but, when engaged with unconsciously, they can dull our awareness and disconnect us from our intentions.

The key is not to eliminate these things from our lives, but instead, engage with them intentionally. For example, if you choose to scroll through social media, set a clear intention as to why you're doing so. Are you seeking inspiration, connection, or relaxation? By bringing awareness to these activities, you reclaim your power and prevent them from pulling you into distraction or autopilot.

As I mentioned in Chapter 1, there are forces that seek to steer humanity toward the timeline of the Great Reset (*page 12*), because fear is profitable. Distractions are deliberately placed in our path, targeting our mindset and habits, to keep us from ever realizing or acting on our true potential. Our attention is a currency and when we're pulled out of presence, we become more susceptible to the noise and become consumed by the superficial, losing sight of our deeper calling. The more we cultivate presence, living in union with intention and flow, the more we align with the timeline of the New Earth.

To live intentionally, we must be present with what's unfolding in and around us – in our environment, our relationships, and our inner world. Presence allows us to pause, to breathe, and to witness all the little moments that make up our lives. For example, consider the simple act of drinking a cup of tea. Without intention, it might just be another mundane task. Instead of mindlessly glugging it down, take a moment to feel the warmth of the cup, inhale the aroma, and savor the taste with each sip. This simple act, performed with intention, becomes a meditation, a moment of connection with yourself and the present. Each small step taken with intention builds upon the last, creating a momentum that can lead to significant changes over time.

Similarly, our communication can be transformed through intention. Choosing our words mindfully, speaking from the heart, and listening deeply to others, are all ways to bring intentionality into our interactions. The Violet Flame can amplify this practice, helping us to clear any discordant energies in our communication and allowing love and authenticity to flow.

There is a delicate dance between the mind and the body when it comes to presence. This is reflective of the inner union we discussed in the previous chapter (*page 90*). The mind is a powerful tool that allows us to navigate life. It helps us analyze, plan, problem-solve, and communicate. However, the mind is also the birthplace of overthinking, judgment, and attachment to thoughts, which can pull us away from the present moment. It's also home to our ego, which can lead us into reliving the past or focusing on the future, which takes us out of presence. Instead of experiencing life as it's happening, we engage with a mental projection of reality based on what could have been or what might be. The past is where our lessons lie and the future is where we're headed, so they are both important to reflect on – however, it's more supportive to spend time engaging with these thoughts intentionally.

The body, on the other hand, is always present. It exists in the here and now – it cannot live in the past or the future. When we connect with the body, we naturally draw our awareness back to the current moment. The light of the Violet Flame invites us into the present, and this holds the space for our intentions to arise naturally. We can drop into our body, and we can listen to the whispers of our heart, guided by the Violet Flame's purifying energy. In this state, our intentions are presented to us by the deeper knowing of our soul, rather than driven by egoic ideals.

To stay in presence, we must root ourselves in the body while being aware of our thoughts. We do require the mind to live intentionally – it allows us to notice what's happening and make conscious choices. The key is using the mind as a tool while you remain anchored in the body.

When we live with intention, even the most ordinary experiences can become an act of devotion to the Self. Washing the dishes becomes a practice of gratitude for the nourishment we've received. A walk in nature becomes an opportunity to connect with the Earth and recharge our energy. This changes our energetic vibration and in turn impacts our reality. These shifts in perspective enhance our relationship with the world around us, allowing us to see the interconnectedness of all things. It invites us to approach life with reverence and wonder, recognizing that every moment is a gift.

Setting Intentions

A powerful ritual for setting intentions with the Violet Flame involves the creation of a vision board. This practice connects the heart and mind while also serving as a tangible reminder of what you're aligning with.

1. Before you begin, create a sacred space as you've done in previous chapters (*for more guidance, see page 16*).

2. Drop into your body to center yourself in the present moment. Sit comfortably, close your eyes, and take several slow, deep breaths. With each exhale, release any tension or thoughts, allowing your awareness to settle into your body. Bring your attention to your heart center. Place your hands over your heart if it's comfortable to do so and connect to the Violet Flame gently glowing here, radiating warmth and love.

3. Ask yourself:

    + Where does my heart guide me?

    + What intentions feel aligned with my soul's highest calling?

4. Rather than forcing an answer, allow your intentions to arise naturally, like a whisper or a feeling that expands in your chest. Trust whatever comes forward, even if it's subtle.

5. Stay present with your breath and the sensations in your body. By residing in your heart space, the more authentic and aligned your intentions will feel. Remember, we're allowing them to arise naturally.

6. With a clear and open heart, now gather materials to create your vision board. You can use magazines, printed images, drawings, or even handwritten affirmations that reflect the intentions you wish to align with.

7. Begin to add them to your board and take your time with this step, remaining present as you select images and words. Each choice and placement is an act of intention, a reflection of what you're inviting into your life. Focus on how or what you want to feel, embody, or create – it could be bliss, expansion, gentleness, strength, abundance, freedom, purpose, or love. As you place each image or word on your board, take a moment to connect with the energy it represents.

8. Once your vision board is complete, light a violet candle. Hold your vision board to your heart (or place it in front of you) and visualize the Violet Flame surrounding it. See its light infusing each image, word, and intention with its vibrant violet energy, amplifying their power and aligning them with your highest good. Take a moment to feel the energy of the Violet Flame, as it strengthens the connection between you and the intentions on your board. You may wish to say:

> *'I charge these intentions with the transformative energy of the Violet Flame. I align with my highest good and the highest good of all. I trust in the divine flow of creation.'*

9. Now speak your intentions aloud. As you do, feel them radiating from your heart space, as though they're already manifesting in your life. Use confident, clear, and affirmative language, and infuse each statement with gratitude for their unfolding.

10. Place your vision board somewhere you'll see it regularly, so it will serve as a daily reminder of the intentions you've set. Every time you see your vision board, take a moment to reconnect with your intentions and the Violet Flame. You can do this by simply placing your hand on your heart, taking a deep breath, and visualizing violet light surrounding you.

When we live with intention, we reclaim our power as conscious creators of our reality. We move through life as active, empowered beings.

When we begin to live intentionally, we move out from perfectionism and control. We practice presence instead so we can listen more deeply, recognizing that every thought, every action, and every moment holds the potential for transformation. And as the Violet Flame anchors us in the present, we can make choices from the heart that will align us with our highest timeline and manifest a life that reflects the deepest truth of who we are.

Source Not Force

When we release the need to force outcomes or control situations, and instead attune ourselves to the universal rhythm, we step into a state of grace where synchronicity becomes our guiding compass. This is such an expansive state of being, where we experience pure ease.

Setting intentions is an act of empowerment, as is the moment we declare to the universe our desires, dreams, and aspirations. When intentions are born from a place of purity – a space where our heart's desires resonate with our soul's truth – they carry the frequency of Source energy. This resonance creates a magnetic field that begins to draw to us the people, opportunities, and circumstances that support our path. It's the difference between setting intentions rooted in egoic desires, which often lead to struggle and resistance, and those grounded in a deep knowing of our divine mission.

The universe speaks to us in whispers, subtle nudges, and spectacles of synchronicity. These synchronistic events are not mere coincidences, they are the language of creation.

> 'There are no such things as coincidences, creation is far too intelligent for that.'
> **Unknown**

Synchronicities can show up as unexpected encounters, repeated symbols, or a sudden feeling of clarity in a moment of doubt. Recognizing and following these signs is an act of trust – as quite often they're only given one step at a time. We must surrender to the mystery, as the path only unfolds as we walk it. Trust is an act of courage, and the Violet Flame ignites this within us.

Sometimes, synchronicities appear as confirmations, a gentle reassurance from the universe that we're on the right track. A chance meeting with someone who offers a word of encouragement or presents an opportunity, a book that seemingly 'falls' into our hands and has a profound message that landed at exactly the right time, or a song that answers a question we've been asking. These moments affirm that we're aligning with Source energy – these are cosmic winks.

Yet it's important to note that synchronicities don't always arrive in grand or dramatic ways. Often, they're very subtle, requiring us to cultivate presence and awareness to notice them. The more we tune in to the rhythm of life, the more these moments of alignment will reveal themselves.

In contrast to the effortless flow of creation, trying to force outcomes creates resistance. When we push too hard, cling too tightly, or try to control every detail of our journey, we disconnect from the ease that we get to experience when in a flow state. This approach is often born out of fear – fear of the unknown, fear of failure, or fear of surrendering to something that's felt and not always seen. Forcing is rooted in lack, the belief that we must manipulate circumstances to achieve our desires. This mindset not only drains our energy, it also blinds us to the synchronicities and opportunities that are already present. The more we force, the more we struggle, and the further we drift from the ease and abundance that comes from aligning with universal love.

However, as we align with this energy of universal love, we step into the realm of infinite potential. We begin to see how each moment presents us with countless timelines and possibilities that can unfold based on the choices we make and the vibrational frequency we emit.

There's a beautiful paradox in this dance of cocreation, this union: While we hold the power to influence our reality, we control nothing. The more we try to grasp and control, the more elusive our desires become. True mastery lies in embracing this paradox, understanding that our role is to align with love and act from a place of inspired intention, while also trusting the greater orchestration of the universe. This paradox teaches us that everything matters, yet nothing matters. Every choice we make ripples outward, impacting the collective, yet the infinite nature of creation ensures that there's always another opportunity, another timeline, another moment to choose differently. This perspective dissolves the illusion of lack and reminds us that we're already whole.

When we direct the Violet Flame toward our intentions, we amplify their vibrational frequency, ensuring they resonate with the highest good. The Flame also acts as a light, illuminating the synchronicities that guide our path and helping us recognize the subtle signs of what we're aligning to.

I've experienced countless synchronicities, some so subtle they weave seamlessly into daily life, while others have been so undeniable it felt as if the universe had thrown a lightning bolt straight at me, there was no missing them. When you awaken to magic, synchronicity becomes the norm, yet it never loses its wonder. Each time it appears it fills me with awe. No matter how often it happens, it's never something I take for granted, and I always feel so humbled when I experience it.

✦

One of the most profound synchronicities of my life unfolded shortly after returning from Thailand, where I'd rewritten my story with my dad (*as I shared in Chapter 4, page 80*). Stepping back into my two-bedroom house, I was struck with an undeniable truth – it no longer fit me. I'd just spent three weeks traveling with nothing but the essentials on my back, and I hadn't missed a single thing from my home. Suddenly, everything inside felt like just 'stuff.' More than that, I realized I was working endlessly in corporate leadership roles to essentially pay for it all... What was I doing?!

I was extremely grateful for my home, filled with beauty, adorned with crystals, art, and plants, each piece carrying meaning. Yet, deep within, I felt an intense calling to release it all. My intuition ignited a certainty, and I could feel the Violet Flame burning within me, urging me to find the courage to transform my life radically. The message was clear: time to evolve – sell the house.

Within weeks, I did just that. I either sold or gifted most of my belongings and purchased a campervan. I had no idea what I was doing, but I kept trusting, moving forward, surrendering to the flow. Doors opened, guides appeared, support arrived, and I was even offered a park-up pitch at a campsite, giving me a stable place to adjust in once my house sold.

Two weeks before handing over the keys, my best friends surprised me with a birthday weekend retreat. As part of the celebration, they held a 'Closing the Bones' ceremony, a ritual to honor all I had released and to support my rebirth into the new way of being. Before the ceremony, I pulled a card from Rebecca Campbell's *Work Your Light Oracle Cards*. The card was 'Awakening – Energetic upgrades. A new way of being. Integration.'

I laughed. As a devoted student of the Gene Keys (Richard Rudd's profound system that shares practical wisdom to guide you to your higher purpose), I knew that Gene Key 51 – 'Awakening,' was the very lesson I was here to learn. It was written in my chart as my deepest area of growth.

Moving day arrived. I was overwhelmed with emotion; this house had been my sanctuary, a place that had held me through heartbreak and healing. I knew I couldn't cling to what it had been. Seeking comfort, I pulled another oracle card from *Work Your Light* (the first since my birthday). Again, I drew the 'Awakening' card. I smiled. A little nod from Source, reminding me I was exactly where I was meant to be.

Then, the final synchronicity. As I arrived at the new community space, I reversed my van onto the allocated pitch. My friend knocked on the back doors and held up the pitch number sign. Pitch 51. The same number as the Awakening Gene Key – the lesson my soul came here to embody! In that moment, I felt the entire universe cheering me on. I'd listened to my intuition, set my intention, followed the synchronistic breadcrumbs, and found myself in the vortex of divine flow.

This is what happens when we ignite the Violet Flame within us, listen to the whispers of our soul, surrender into trust, and act with courage (becoming the Unified Flame). As we walk this path of union, we transform our own lives while contributing to the collective awakening.

Living Magic

Throughout this chapter we've discussed a significant paradox: We are both creators and passengers of our reality. We set intention, and we surrender to what is. When we align with our soul's intentions and the greater rhythm of the universe, we open the door to a life that feels deeply enchanting, and realize magic is, and always has been, right here!

With this alignment, any threads of needing to cling to control or anything that emerges from the illusion of lack, is transmuted by the Violet Flame. Instead, it refines our connection to the unseen realms, allowing us to shift between frequencies, unlock codes, awaken deep knowing, and receive the guiding whispers of intuition. Magic, in this sense, isn't separate from us. It's our natural state, a flow that we step into when we let go of resistance and trust. When we live with magic as the default, we're no longer confined to a linear existence. Instead, we awaken to the interconnectedness of all things and the miracles that arise from this union.

When we come into deeper presence, living intentionally while having a reverence for the synchronicities, they then multiply. It's as though the universe responds to our awareness by offering more breadcrumbs to guide us. This attunement to the subtle language of creation opens us to the infinite possibilities available.

To live a magical life, we must strengthen our connection to intuition and fine-tune our ability to sense energy. Everything we perceive, from the densest physical matter to the subtlest whispers of intuition, is vibrating energy. We exist within a vast cosmic highway, an infinite field of energy that holds all information, wisdom, and potential throughout all of time and space. It's not something separate from us; we're moving through it and it's moving through us. The signal is constantly present, woven like golden threads that stretch across all of creation, linking every moment, every being, and every possibility. These threads form fractal pathways – these are the patterns within creation that mirror and repeat – allowing us to move through different dimensions of awareness.

Just as a radio must be tuned to the right frequency to pick up a signal, we too can attune ourselves to different energetic fields. When we consciously tune in to this cosmic highway, we realize that all wisdom is accessible. Every thought, every emotion, every experience, ripples across these energetic threads, influencing the way we interact with the universe. The more we refine our vibration, the clearer the signals become, and the more effortlessly we can navigate the unseen realms of energy, intuition, and creation, which brings more ease to our lives. I call this having a strong 'third eye Wi-Fi'.

To develop our 'third eye Wi-Fi' requires us to be fully grounded. We can only successfully jump into the cosmic highway if we're anchored in the body. True intuition is a mix of receiving guidance and knowing what to trust through having fine-tuned discernment. The Violet Flame can assist us in grounding and setting boundaries to create a safe container for the magic, ensuring that our energy remains potent, clearing the way for intuition.

Discernment is key as we open ourselves – we must cultivate the ability to distinguish between true guidance and external noise. Without discernment, we can easily be swayed by illusions, fear-based narratives, or even our own unprocessed emotions masquerading as intuition. Your body is a finely tuned instrument for discernment. Notice how you physically respond to people, situations, and information. Does something feel expansive and light, or does it create tension and resistance? Trust these signals. Before accepting information, ask: Does this resonate deeply with my soul? Does it empower me, or does it create fear and dependency? Is this coming from love or from distortion? You can always consciously connect with the Violet Flame to assist this process.

By strengthening discernment, we create healthy, energetic boundaries, ensuring that we're not blindly absorbing information. This allows us to navigate the cosmic currents with confidence, knowing that we're receiving insight from a place of light. In developing intuition, discernment is the guardian that keeps us anchored in truth.

From the space of union and flow, miracles become a natural part of our experience. Living magic is an invitation to step into the fullness of who you are. It brings moments of wonder to things you may have previously perceived as mundane, you transcend boredom, lack, feeling unsafe – it all dissipates. When you choose to live with magic as the default, you transform your life; you inspire others to do the same. Together, we cocreate a world where miracles are the norm, and the Violet Flame burns brightly uniting us all.

Connecting with Intuition

In this practice, the Violet Flame supports you to awaken and sharpen your intuitive senses, to attune to the divine flow, and strengthen your 'third eye Wi-Fi.' It can be helpful to connect to the energies of Archangel Zadkiel and Holy Amethyst as they offer their wings of light, which can assist with creating a protective container.

Remember to take a deep breath and gently ground yourself before you begin, so you feel anchored in your body and to the earth. Connect with the Violet Flame in a way that feels most nurturing for you (for further guidance, see page 18).

Practice to Strengthen Discernment

Part of developing intuition is learning what to trust. The Violet Flame helps us discern truth from illusion and create healthy, energetic boundaries.

1. Visualize a shield of violet fire forming around your entire body – the Flame transmutes denser vibrations and transforms them in to pure light.

2. Feel the Flame spinning around you, refining your energy, sharpening your perception, and creating a clear distinction

between your own energy and any influences or vibrations you choose not to align to.

3. As you hold this vision, place your hands over your heart and breathe deeply.

4. If any energies feel heavy or intrusive, see the Violet Flame burning them away, and feel the wings of light retaining the purity of your energy field. Say aloud or silently:

> 'With the Violet Flame, I create clear and sovereign, energetic boundaries. I can discern truth from illusion, wisdom from noise. I align only to that which is for my highest good and the highest good of all.'

Practice to Awaken the Third Eye

Next, we awaken and attune our third eye Wi-Fi – our inner vision and intuitive knowing so that we may receive guidance with clarity and trust.

1. Bring your awareness to your third eye, the space between your eyebrows.

2. Imagine a soft, violet light forming in this area, pulsing with warmth and energy.

3. Call upon Archangel Zadkiel and Holy Amethyst, asking them to wrap their wings of light around you. Feel their presence as they extend their radiant, shimmering wings, gently cocooning you.

4. As you breathe deeply, see their wings infusing your being with light, expanding your ability to see, sense, and perceive beyond the physical realm. Say aloud or silently:

'My third eye is clear. Let me see beyond illusion, hear beyond words, and feel beyond the seen. My intuition is sharp, and I am guided by the highest truth.'

Practice to Connect to Intuition

Now that your third eye is open and clear, and your boundaries are strong, it's time to listen for any guidance that wishes to come through.

1. Sit in stillness and allow your breath to flow naturally.

2. Ask the Violet Flame: 'What wisdom do you have for me today?'

3. Observe any images, words, sensations, or feelings that arise. Trust what you receive, even if it comes as a whisper, a subtle knowing.

4. If nothing comes immediately, that's OK. The message may come later as a synchronicity, a dream, or an intuitive nudge.

5. When you feel complete, gently bring your awareness back to your body, wiggling your fingers and toes. Thank Archangel Zadkiel, Holy Amethyst, and the Violet Flame for their guidance and support. Say aloud or silently:

    'I am clear, centered, and attuned to the wisdom of my soul. My third eye sees with clarity, my heart listens with love, and my path is illuminated by the Violet Flame.'

Closing the Space After the Practice

1. Take a moment to journal any insights or feelings that came through during the practice. If you wish, anoint your third eye

with essential oil (such as frankincense or lavender) to seal in the energy. If you lit a candle to support you with connecting to the Violet Flame, extinguish it with gratitude, knowing that the Violet Flame will continue to be with you, ongoing.

2. Drink a glass of water to ground yourself, bringing the magic of this practice fully into your physical reality.

By working with the Violet Flame, Archangel Zadkiel, and Holy Amethyst, you've activated a powerful gateway to divine insight. Your 'third eye Wi-Fi' is now more attuned, your intuition more receptive, and your discernment more defined.

As you move forward, notice how your awareness shifts. Do synchronicities appear more often? Are intuitive messages coming through with greater clarity? Trust that this practice has set a frequency in motion, one that will continue to unfold in the days and weeks ahead.

CHAPTER 7

Igniting Higher Purpose

'You are a spark of infinite creation,'
the Violet Flame flickered. 'Within you lies
a divine blueprint, a melody only you can sing,
a path only you can walk. You ignite your higher
purpose in remembering who you are.'

I felt the glow of the violet light swirl around me,
'How do I live that purpose?' I asked.
'Even in the moments I'm bound by self-doubt?'

The Violet Flame danced brighter,
'Your doubts are just the shadows of forgotten truths,'
it replied. 'And I am here to burn them away.
When you live with me as your guiding frequency,
you clear the residue of old karma, untangle the threads
of past choices, and open the door to a new reality.
Timelines are pliable, ever-shifting streams of possibility.
Each thought, word, and action ripples out as creation,
crafting your next chapter. You are beginning to see
how you are the architect of your own becoming.'

I found these words both liberating and humbling.
'How do I choose?' I whispered. 'With so many possibilities,
how do I know which one is meant for me?'

The Flame shimmered softly, its violet hue pulsing gently.
'Do not seek the "right" way, for there is no single way.
Instead, align with the truth of your heart, and the
path that reflects your essence will reveal itself.
Your purpose is not what you do, it is who you are:
Love. Speak your reality into existence with the power of
I AM: a sacred spell that attunes you to the vibration
of creation itself. Each time you embody I AM,
you experience a timeline of your choosing.'

I felt a lump in my throat, as if I had forgotten
the power of my voice. 'How do I reclaim it?' I asked,
'This essence of who I AM truly, who I AM here to 'be'?'

The Violet Flame blazed brighter,
wrapping me in its transformative light.
'Speak, and know you are heard by the universe,'
it said. 'Your voice is a conduit of divinity,
a unique tone that resonates through the cosmos.
When you express yourself fully, you reclaim
the sovereignty that has always been yours.'

I placed my hand on my heart, feeling the resonance of
the Violet Flame settle within me. 'What if I falter?'
I asked softly. 'Or make choices that lead me astray?'

The Flame softened, its glow enveloping me.
'Even in faltering, you are still creating,' it replied.
'Remember this paradox: that free will and fate both exist
simultaneously, so there is no such thing as being lost –
there is only exploration. And when you return to me,
I will always be here to guide you back to your center.
Remember, you are never separate from creation,
and each moment holds the potential to begin anew.'

And as its glow settled into my core I knew,
the Violet Flame was no longer just a fire to call upon,
it was a frequency to live by. Through it, I could
clear karmic residue, be in my full expression,
embody love, and have the courage to play
within the infinite possibilities of creation.

At the heart of fully embracing our purpose comes the understanding that we're both creators and creations, weaving our lives through choices, actions, and vibration. The Violet Flame, with its alchemical frequency, offers a way to dissolve the denser energetic imprints that cloud our perception of what we truly are (which is universal love) and instead express ourselves freely.

In each moment, we can transform the reality we experience as timelines are fluid, infinite and continuously changing. With each choice we can either embody love or align to fear, and this is where we find purpose. There is a misconception that our purpose is a role we must fulfill. When actually purpose is in the 'being' and not the 'doing': being and embodying the essence of all encompassing love in our own unique way.

Purpose is the expression of your soul's truth in each moment, the courage to live unapologetically as your authentic self. By connecting with the Violet Flame and harnessing the I AM Presence, you ignite the path forward, creating experiences that are uniquely yours to explore.

Karmic Shift

Karma, in its essence, refers to the principle of cause and effect: the idea that our thoughts, actions, and intentions create energetic imprints that shape our experiences over time. It's an accumulation of energy we've put out into the world returning to us. Our vibration is like a magnetic signal that attracts back to us more of the same frequency.

As we harness the Violet Flame, it dissolves the dense, stagnant energies tied to past actions, thoughts, emotions, and experiences that make up our karmic imprints. It doesn't erase karma, as each action has its effect, but instead shifts and transforms the emotional energetics tied to karmic residues, changing the pathway forward.

As already shared in Chapter 4, when we forgive ourselves and the people around us, our physical reality literally starts to shift right in front of our eyes. This is because we're not only freeing ourselves from the past when we embody forgiveness, we're also changing our personal karma. When we forgive and heal, we reshape our emotional response to the past, effectively neutralizing any karmic residue that these memories or patterns may have previously held over us. In doing so, we move out from recurring negative cycles, clearing our karmic 'debt,' and enabling us to enter timelines that bring pathways to new, more aligned possibilities. Essentially, we've opened the door for new opportunities to appear that didn't exist within our previous reality, as we hadn't aligned to them vibrationally.

Karma can also be carried over from past lives as our spirit is eternal. Some spiritual teachings suggest that we experience multiple lives through different physical bodies. In the ethereal planes, we each have an 'Akashic record' – a memory of the entirety of all our experiences throughout all our lifetimes. Each incarnation presents us with different opportunities for soul growth, intended for us to learn lessons and come to karmic resolution. Through this process the soul expands and evolves until reaching a state of completion, merging fully back to oneness where it no longer reincarnates as physical form. Many people experience karmic influences from their past lives in their current life, such as certain phobias, recurring relationship issues, or irrational fears that seem to have no basis in their current life.

With the Violet Flame, we can acknowledge and heal these past-life experiences, sending forgiveness back to our past lives, and dissolving any unresolved energies that may have 'carried over.' In the next practice, we'll revisit the Temple of the Violet Flame, so you can receive a transmission from Archangel Zadkiel to clear karmic residues you might still be carrying.

Clearing Karmic Residues

1. Prepare yourself a sacred space so you can drop into this practice fully, ensuring you won't be disturbed. Remember to take a deep breath and gently ground yourself so you feel anchored. Set the intention for this practice: to clear past-life karma by sending the Violet Flame through time and space. *(For more preparation guidance, see page 16).*

2. With your next inhale, visualize a path before you leading up to a grand temple shimmering with violet light. As you walk closer

to it, feel the gentle warmth and purifying energy of the Violet Flame surrounding the temple. The temple walls are glistening with amethyst, and you can see prisms of rainbow light shining through the air.

3. As you approach, feel a sense of returning home, as if your soul has walked through this entrance many times before. The doors of the temple open gently, inviting you inside. You step across the threshold into a sanctuary of profound peace, and you drop into complete presence. The amethyst walls pulse with light, and at the center, the Violet Flame burns brightly – alive, transformative, yet gentle. Its light dances on the walls, illuminating the temple with a gold and violet light.

4. In the glow of the Flame stands Archangel Zadkiel, his presence radiant and comforting, eyes filled with compassion and acceptance. He greets you with a soft smile and gestures for you to step forward. As you draw nearer, you feel pure, universal love – being in this energy may bring up some emotion; allow it to flow. Archangel Zadkiel places his hands over your heart, and a surge of warmth moves through you. You feel the depth of all karmic residues lifting from your being as an overwhelming sense of forgiveness opens up your heart to the frequency of pure compassion. Archangel Zadkiel offers a decree for you to declare:

'By the grace of Divine Love, I call forth the Violet Flame to cleanse and transmute all karmic residues across past, present, and future timelines. I embrace the purity of my soul's truth and reclaim my sovereign power. As I embody the essence of universal love, I align with my highest purpose. And so it is.'

5. Breathe deeply, allowing these words to settle into every cell. Visualize the Violet Flame expanding, dissolving shadows,

cleansing your past-life imprints, and transmuting them into radiant love. Feel the liberation of your energy, sovereign and free.

6. Archangel Zadkiel then hands you a book bound in violet and gold, your Akashic record. As you open it, you find the pages blank, awaiting your intention. This is your opportunity to rewrite your story.

7. See a golden quill appear in your hand, and across these empty pages, begin to envision a future timeline: one where you're fully empowered, clear of all karmic attachments, living in alignment with your truest self. Who are you with an empty page, without anything holding you back from your true expression? How do you share your gifts and love without hesitation? What does your life look like when you create from a space of universal love and freedom? Allow your heart to create.

8. When you feel complete, take a moment to thank Archangel Zadkiel for his healing energy and the Violet Flame for its transformative power. Express gratitude to yourself for embarking on this journey of karmic clearing.

9. Set the intention that going forward you are beginning again. Each word, thought, action will be from a place of love.

10. Slowly begin to bring your awareness back to the room, feeling the ground beneath you and the air around you.

11. Take a few deep breaths, knowing that you've brought about karmic shifts, not only for yourself but for your ancestors and future generations.

Beautifully Becoming

A shift is happening, a transformation rippling through us collectively. Humanity has moved so far into the vibration of separation that we've forgotten entirely what we are, and our sense of purpose has become somewhat lost at this time of amnesia. However, a great awakening is happening. The old structures, built on fear, separation, and scarcity, are dissolving, making way for a new era. This is a time of spiritual progression, where we're invited to move beyond conditioned ways of thinking and instead ignite purpose through living our most authentic expression.

As part of the collective awakening, we're no longer going along with the status quo or blindly following what's broadcast via the media as 'truth.' We're beginning to ask questions and instead tune in to our own inner knowing.

There is one fundamental question at the core of this awakening: 'Who am I here to be?'

This question carries the collective memory that flows through our veins. The further we stray from our natural state, the more we begin to remember the true meaning of life. This question is not about what you should 'do' but rather about who you 'are' at the purest level – beyond expectation, beyond conditioning, beyond limitation. When you surrender to this question, you begin to see that purpose is not a destination, a job title, or based upon external validation.

Purpose is the essence of who we are when we are fully expressed, when we feel alive, when we live free by bringing our authentic presence to everything we do. Our expression is our unique gift to the world; it becomes our service. So when we share our expression, it always comes with the knowing that we are living our purpose.

> *'The meaning of life is to find your gift.
> The purpose of life is to give it away.'*
> PABLO PICASSO

As you continue through this book and integrate the Violet Flame as both a tool to assist you and a frequency to live by, you're courageously stepping into your highest potential. And you'll be shifted into navigating the timeline of your most expanded, authentic self – thus, living your purpose.

✦

My intention in starting to write this book was to clear years of writer's block and reclaim my voice – to transform the belief that it was unsafe to write things down. Putting this manuscript out in the world was a breakthrough moment. I'd rewritten my story, alchemized the fear, and freed my voice. I had expressed myself fully, in my truth through my written words.

Three months later, I received a call offering me a publishing contract. Within an hour of that call, my line manager at the charity I worked for phoned to say my role was being made redundant. I couldn't believe the timing and how everything was unfolding – the universe was creating the way for me! One timeline was ending, and a new one was opening up right before my eyes, happening in real time. As a result of sharing my most authentic expression, I was about to become a published author.

Looking back, I see how following my gut, trusting the signs, and surrendering to the unknown led me to fulfilling my purpose, which was to be in my heart expression and true to my authentic self. The Violet Flame was with me throughout the entire process, not only transforming my experience in that moment, but assisting me through the series of events that led me here. It had been my guiding light through my whole life. I remembered that my soul came here to serve, to share, to guide others through their own rebirth.

In this moment of reflection, I could see the bigger picture – how my lived experiences and my willingness to embrace transformation through connecting with the Violet Flame had all contributed to this point. I had stepped into a new timeline; one where I was living my higher purpose, completely free to write this book and share the transformative power of the Violet Flame. By choosing to live authentically and express myself fully, a whole new reality was created.

Our higher purpose often reveals itself through the courage to follow the subtle, intuitive nudges, to trust the divine timing of our lives, and to say 'yes' to the unknown. In doing so, we align with the flow of the universe, stepping into the life our soul has always known was possible. Your authentic expression is your gift to the world. It's already here, waiting for permission to be felt, moved, spoken, danced. It's the breath of your soul and the truth of your being translated into form.

The Violet Flame purifies the residue of fear that silences your voice, contracts your body, and dims your spirit. It softens the armor you built to survive in a world that asked you to shrink back or play small. It reminds us that we're not here to be a copy of anyone else. We're not here to perform a version of ourselves that pleases others. We're here to express the frequency of our soul, just as it is. All masks removed.

The Violet Flame shows us that we don't need to fix ourselves to be worthy of expression. We don't have to have it all figured out to express ourselves. We express to free what's been trapped, and in doing so, we discover who we truly are. This is the beauty of becoming. A moment-to-moment unfolding of expression.

Dancing with the Violet Flame

One of the most powerful ways to activate our fullest expression is through the body. Our bodies are vessels of wisdom, encoded with knowing. When we move with presence, we unlock deeper levels of truth – not through *thinking* our way, instead through *feeling* it. This practice invites you to step into the Violet Flame as an embodied experience. Here, movement becomes a portal, a way of communing with your essence and allowing your expression to emerge.

1. Begin by creating a playlist that resonates with your soul – songs that ignite your spirit, evoke freedom, and anchor you in the present. (If you're unsure of creating your own, you can go to YouTube or SoundCloud and type into the search box, 'Light up my soul', to choose a pre-made playlist.)

2. Prepare your space so it feels clear, open, and safe for expression. Ground yourself with a few deep breaths and set a clear intention: to connect with the Violet Flame and to unlock your most authentic Self through the medium of movement.

3. As the music begins, tune in to the sound and notice how your body instinctively wants to move. This practice is about being how you want to be through the movement. If you notice any need to perform or control, shake it off and tune back in to how your heart wants to move you. The sound is the anchor; feel the rhythm, letting it pulse through your body.

4. Invoke the Violet Flame with intention:

> *'I connect with the Violet Flame, burn brightly through me now. Transform all that restricts me from being in authenticity and, instead, I surrender into presence. I am ready to move and be moved. I am ready to embody my essence and express my truth.'*

5. Let these words ripple through you, awakening the fire within. Move freely and instinctively, whether it's swaying, stretching, spinning, or shaking. If you encounter heaviness, shake it out. If you feel stiff, breathe deeply, inviting flow. If you feel expansive, reach for the sky, twirl, stretch, express it fully. Trust that your body knows exactly how to release and activate. Let yourself be led by the Violet Flame, each movement unlocking deeper levels of authentic expression within you.

6. Imagine the Violet Flame igniting every cell and sense it alchemizing old patterns, dissolving restrictions. Feel yourself shifting so you can live your purpose through liberation, authenticity, and being free in your expression.

7. When the movement naturally slows, come to a place of stillness. Sit or lie down, place your hands over your heart, and breathe deeply.

8. Ask yourself:

    ✦ What did I feel during this practice?

    ✦ What messages came through?

    ✦ How can I embody my essence and express myself more fully in my daily life?

9. Write any insights in a journal, allowing your intuition to speak. This practice is an initiation; each time you return to it, you deepen your connection to your authentic expression. Embrace this practice regularly, and watch as it transforms how you move, express, and live, rooted in truth, ignited by your purpose to 'be.'

I AM

There's a pure consciousness that resides within each of us; a quintessence that is eternal and limitless. An unchanging, infinite essence that simply 'is.' This spark of divinity, the very spirit of creation flowing through our being, is known in the teachings of Saint Germain as the 'I AM Presence.'

When we connect with the vibration of I AM, it removes us from ego mind and drops us entirely into a state of pure being, which is our higher purpose – simply 'to be.' In the day-to-day, our thoughts and perceptions can fragment our realities as we project them onto what's being experienced. However, the moment we speak 'I AM,' we bring ourselves fully into the present moment, free from the illusions of past or future, just a pure stream of consciousness.

In this state of presence, we're only with what 'is' – neither attaching nor projecting anything to it, we're actively perceiving the present moment without identification or judgment. Awareness and consciousness merge, so we're further unified and there's no separation between the one who is aware and the essence of consciousness itself. It's an experience of pure, undivided presence, union, peace… this is where universal love resides. Here, we get a glimpse of non-duality; the realization that beneath all layers of identity and separation lies the purity of I AM. This is our infinite nature – whole, complete, and requiring nothing.

Across all religions and spiritual traditions, this recognition of a simple state of being (pure awareness) is a common thread that connects all and resonates as truth. It's undeniable, irrespective of whatever path, teaching, or practices you follow. This is why the I AM Presence is so much more than a philosophy, it's a living, breathing embodiment of truth. It calls us home to ourselves.

Saint Germain emphasizes that the I AM Presence is our direct connection to creation. When he walked the Earth, he taught that whenever we declare 'I AM,' we're speaking the name of 'God.' According to Exodus 3:14, when Moses asked for God's name, the answer was 'I AM THAT I AM.'

The foundation of Saint Germain's teachings is that we're not separate from God. Instead, we're all one. We're a creation of God, and God creates through us. Of course, you can replace the word God with whatever feels right to you – Source, the universe, Divine Beloved, etc. The key is that there's no separation – and the concept that anything is separate from the Self is illusion.

Saint Germain shares that when we speak 'I AM,' we're directly connecting to the creative energy that flows through all. By recognizing and embodying this I AM Presence, we can step into our full divine potential and manifest miracles.

He also teaches that spoken word is one of our greatest tools for creation and manifestation. Sound is a conduit for energy, and our voice is the bridge between thought and form. Everything in the universe vibrates, and sound is the fabric of the universe. Our voice carries our unique energetic imprint, resonating at a frequency that influences our own field and the space around us. When we speak, we're quite literally shaping reality through sound.

This is why using your voice is so crucial to your wellbeing. The words you use and also the energy behind them – the tone, the resonance, the truth carried in each syllable. Many ancient traditions understood this, using mantras, chants, and sacred sounds to shift consciousness, to bring about healing, and alter vibrational states. Sound frequencies influence cellular processes through resonance, where certain vibrations can stimulate cells to release stress, to repair, and regenerate.

To embody our creative essence and expression we must reclaim our voice, both literally and metaphorically. When we suppress our truth, when we silence our intuition, when we withhold our authentic expression, we disconnect from our innate power, closing the cage door and suffocating our life force. When we speak from our soul, when we allow our unique vibration to move through us unhindered, we are liberated and free, we are one with what is, and we awaken the I AM Presence within.

When we speak 'I AM' with conviction, we activate the sacred geometry of our being, setting into motion the frequencies that begin to shape our reality and giving way for expansion. This is because I AM is the state of pure awareness that all experience is born from. By affirming this we can literally visit the void of creation, the place where anything is possible in any moment. This is why I AM affirmations are so powerful, because they invoke, and then our sound amplifies the intention.

What follows the words 'I AM' is an energetic decree, a direct instruction to the universe. The subconscious mind takes everything we say as truth, reinforcing it with every repetition. When we declare, 'I AM strong,' we're not just stating a fact; we're calling strength into being. If we say 'I AM unworthy,' the universe simply responds, 'As you wish.' This is why discernment in our language is so important. The words we speak hold immense power, shaping our reality with every vibration they emit.

'I AM…' is not just a phrase; it's a command to the universe that will set energy into motion. When we use 'I AM' intentionally, we attune ourselves to the frequency of creation, calling forth the truth of who we are. Whether we say 'I AM love,' 'I AM abundant,' or 'I AM radiant light,' we're not just stating something, through repeated affirmation we become it.

The I AM Presence exists beyond time, while the Violet Flame operates simultaneously across all timelines. When we use them together, we can significantly enhance our ability to manifest. The Violet Flame transforms past, present, and future timelines from the perspective of the eternal now. Therefore, if there are energetic distortions, negative programming, or unconscious resistance that slow down or interfere with manifestation, the Violet Flame works to clear these obstacles. By speaking an 'I AM' affirmation while harnessing the power of the Violet Flame, we allow our intentions to manifest more effortlessly.

Saint Germain reminds us:

> *'You are the I AM Presence in action.*
> *Speak as the Divine, and the universe*
> *will move to meet you.'*

Activating the I AM Presence

To deepen your connection to the I AM Presence, you can engage in a powerful practice that combines sound, embodiment, and intention. This exercise will help open your throat chakra, attune your voice to your highest truth, and activate your creative power. Remember to set your space as you've done before (see page 16), ensuring you're grounded, anchored, and have connected to the Violet Flame before you begin.

1. Close your eyes and place your hands over your heart. Inhale deeply and as you exhale, softly speak:

    'Beloved Saint Germain, Keeper of the Violet Flame, I connect with your divine essence. Surround me in the purifying

> flames of violet light. Guide me as I activate my voice and align with the one absolute truth: I AM that I AM.'

2. Place your hands gently over your neck. Take a deep breath and begin to tone the sound 'HAM' (the seed sound for the throat chakra), allowing it to resonate naturally. Feel the vibration in your throat and chest. Repeat this tone seven times, each time with the intention of clearing and energizing your voice.

3. As you tone, you may also like to begin allowing your voice to make sounds intuitively. Play with the different noises and where you feel them resonating within your body. As you do this visualize the Violet Flame swirling around your throat to support your voice in sounding radiant and clear.

4. Now, bring your awareness to your heart center. Imagine a pathway of violet light leading you deep within, to the void, the space of nothingness from which all experience is born. This is the realm of pure potential, the silence between each breath, the stillness from which creation arises. Speak 'I AM.'

5. In this space, you're free from all limitations. You're simply the I AM – pure presence, pure consciousness. Rest here for a few moments, breathing deeply, and allowing yourself to merge with this infinite silence. If you find yourself in the mind or thoughts coming in, continue to affirm 'I AM,' and it will bring you back to a pure state of being.

6. Softly speak:

> 'I AM that I AM. I am pure presence. I am divine expression. I am the voice of truth.'

Feel these words reverberate through your entire being, anchoring the I AM Presence within you. Saint Germain infuses your energy field with the Violet Flame.

7. From this space of pure potential, allow five I AM affirmations to rise naturally from your heart, for your highest good and the highest good of all. These could be qualities you wish to embody or realities you wish to manifest. Trust your intuition as the words form. Write them down if you feel called to do so. Here are some examples:

   + I AM creating the New Earth.

   + I AM the voice of truth.

   + I AM infinite and limitless.

   + I AM aligned with my highest purpose.

   + I AM an expression of love.

8. One by one, speak each affirmation aloud. Allow your voice to flow freely, letting your unique vibration carry the words. Feel the power of each statement anchoring into your energy field, assisted by the Violet Flame and the presence of Saint Germain. To deepen the activation, chant or sing these affirmations, feeling them resonate in your body and ripple out into the universe. Visualize the Violet Flame amplifying and carrying your intentions through the eternal now.

9. When you've completed your affirmations, bring your hands back to your heart and express gratitude:

> '*Thank you, Saint Germain, for your guidance, protection, and love. Thank you, Violet Flame, for your transformation and amplification. I release this practice with gratitude, trusting that all is manifesting for my highest good.*'

10. Take a few deep breaths and wiggle your fingers and toes, grounding back into the present moment. Before you end, speak one final affirmation:

    > '*I AM the voice of my soul, free, clear, aligned with absolute truth and the embodiment of universal love.*'

11. When you're ready, open your eyes, carrying this energy of pure presence and authentic expression forward.

The more we engage with the I AM Presence, the more we embody it. This practice, when done consistently, becomes a way of living and a path of mastering energy. The words we speak shape the world we walk in. When we choose to declare our truth, to align our voice with our divinity, we reclaim our creative ability and live our purpose.

CHAPTER 8

Lighting the Way

'You have long wandered along the path of separation,
yet the way has always been within you,'
the Violet Flame whispered to me.

I closed my eyes, feeling the Flame flicker within my chest.
'There is a shadow of lack that still lingers in me, a belief
that I am not enough, and that there won't be enough.'

The Violet Flame held me in its light. 'Look closely,'
it said. 'There is no end to creation; it spirals infinitely
outward and inward. As galaxies are being born in
the far reaches of the universe, so too are worlds
forming within the smallest particles of your being.
There is no lack. The infinite exists in you, and as you.'

The Flame vibrated through me, I felt it dissolving
the threads of limitation. 'If I am infinite…'
I whispered, 'then what about the pain, the chaos I see
in the world around me? How can I restore freedom,
whilst others are still on a path of struggle?'

The Violet Flame shimmered,
I was in awe of the intricacy of its movement.
'The micro and the macro are reflections of one another,'
it replied. 'What you heal within yourself ripples outward
into the collective. What you offer to the world mirrors
back into your soul. Creation is based upon fractals
and threads of interconnectedness between all.
So when you tend to the flame of your own heart,
you light up the hearts of all beings.'

I felt the truth of these words.
'How do I serve the whole,' I asked,
'when my journey also feels so personal,
facing my own challenge?'

The Flame softened, its light steadying, its warmth spreading as if it were cradling the entire Earth. 'Self-realization is a profound journey that dissolves separation,' it said. 'As you meet yourself fully, your light, your shadow, your joy, your ache – purity arises. This purity is the truth of who you are: an expression of love, and when you embody this type of love, you naturally become of service to others. Your prayers, your intentions, are heard by creation and it responds. Every compassionate thought, every word of kindness, every act of love, ripples out to the whole. Through the quiet, consistent alignment of your daily choices to the path of love, each micro shift in perception, each small surrender, each tender act of trust, these make up the launch pad for a quantum leap. Do not underestimate your actions, no matter how small they seem. And remember: a butterfly flapping its wings in one part of the world can cause a hurricane on the other side of the globe.'

I felt a surge of purpose rising within me,
The Flame dimmed, its presence settling
deeply into my heart. And in that stillness,
I understood: through the Violet Flame, I could
transform myself and also the collective.
My service was to become a living prayer.
This was the New Paradigm.

The path of awakening ultimately leads us to surrender to the eternal Self. There is no beginning and there is no end to us, to this universe, and all that's beyond. Here, any threads of 'lack' dissolve as we can see the way in which creation infinitely weaves. This also mirrors back to us how, as we shift from the preprogrammed perspective that abundance is something to attain, we can begin to understand that abundance is an ever-present frequency we can tune in to.

Through the teachings of the Violet Flame, we come to see that our mission is both simple and profound: to become a walking expression of love. When we begin to really start to live as the embodiment of universal love, we come to the realization that the energy of giving and receiving is the same. When you're living from a heart space with the Violet Flame at the core, the perception shifts from 'What can I take?' to 'How can I give?' By aligning our thoughts, words, and actions with compassion, we light the way for others to do the same. When we hold the Violet Flame as a prayer in our hearts, we extend its light to all beings.

Infinity Gateway

The Violet Flame is infinite, as the Flame is eternal, continuously burning bright. Its light reaches all places, spiraling both inward and outward. This violet light travels through and around all things; as creation creates, the Violet Flame illuminates.

When we try to grasp the concept of infinity with our minds, it often leaves us feeling boggled. The mind by nature is accustomed to boundaries, definitions, rationality, and linear progression. Our human experience is deeply rooted in time and space: days that begin and end, journeys with starting points and destinations, stories with first chapters and final pages, objects that appear to be solid and finite.

The mind, in its continuous attempt to categorize and comprehend, struggles to contain something that cannot be contained. Infinity by its very nature cannot be understood through the lens of limitation. Science looks at the concept of infinity through the endless expansion of the universe, fractal patterns in nature, and the idea that energy cannot be created or destroyed – only transformed. The very fact that we can contemplate infinity means that it's within our reality, as some part of us remembers it. Infinity becomes something we begin to sense as we remember the eternal Self and the emergence of an inner knowing that creation has no end. To begin to intuit this, we must go beyond the mind and drop into the heart.

Unlike the mind, the heart understands infinity as an experience without the need to grasp it as a concept. Through connecting with the Violet Flame and having moments of profound presence, we catch glimpses of this expanse. For me,

I experience infinity most when I'm looking up at the stars in the sky or gazing out at the ocean to the horizon. The concept of infinity isn't limited to the vastness of outer space, though – it exists equally in the microcosm within us. Just as the universe expands infinitely outward, it also retracts infinitely inward. The same divine intelligence that governs the galaxies also designs the intricate patterns of our cells.

The micro and macro reflect each other in perfect harmony. The branching of rivers as they carve through the land mirrors the web of veins and arteries that flow through the human body, both carrying the essence of life, water and blood, to nourish the whole. The roots of a tree stretch deep into the earth, mirroring the bronchi of human lungs. Just as trees breathe in carbon dioxide and exhale oxygen, our lungs do the opposite, forming an exchange of life force between the inner and outer worlds. The way a single cell divides and expands to create an entire human body mirrors the way stars are born within nebulae, clustering together to form galaxies. Both follow the blueprint of divine expansion and creation. The rhythmic pulse of a human heart mirrors the rise and fall of ocean waves, each one a continuous ebb and flow, reminding us that all of existence moves in cycles of contraction and expansion. The double helix of DNA, which encodes the blueprint of all life, reflects the Fibonacci spiral found in flowers, pine cones, hurricanes, and galaxies, showing that the same sacred geometry shapes life on all scales.

When we grasp this mirroring, it dissolves the illusion of lack, as it reveals a universe that's both infinitely abundant and self-sustaining. We see that lack can't exist in a universe built on infinite expansion and perpetual creation. In every moment, life is continuously generating new possibilities, and by aligning with this flow, we can access the limitless abundance that is our birthright.

Yet lack can be so deeply seeded within. All lack stems from the perceived separation from Source/God/creation, from the earth, from each other, and even from ourselves. In the Western world, where we're often told that there's never enough – time, money, love, or even worth – it's easy to fall into a scarcity mindset.

We're conditioned to believe that life is a series of limitations, where resources are finite, and where we must compete for everything. It leads us to seek safety, security, and comfort in external things: possessions, status, relationships, locations. For when we believe that we're separate from Source, we also naturally fall into the illusion that what we need must come from outside ourselves. This belief fuels a relentless pursuit of 'more' – more money, more approval, more safety, more control, which keeps us locked in cycles of insufficiency.

The Violet Flame calls us forward to step through the Infinity Gateway into a new paradigm. One where the limitations we previously placed upon ourselves and our experience evolve into the knowing that the very nature of creation is limitless. By expanding our awareness and activating our inner vision, we can glimpse the eternal, ever-present flow of energy that's available to us. Through this lens, we come to understand that lack is a misunderstanding of our own divine nature.

If there's no beginning and no end, then the concept of lack simply can't exist. Eternity implies an infinite supply of energy, possibilities, and expression. When we anchor into the truth of our eternal nature, we transcend the fear of running out, whether that's time, money, resources, or love.

This shift in perception dissolves the scarcity thinking. The fear that we must compete or hoard to survive loses its grip, replaced by an inner knowing that we're always provided for. The Violet Flame alchemizes the unconscious imprints of lack and transforms them into an abundance frequency. It dissipates the limiting beliefs stored within our energy field, which then shifts us into a reality where we trust the infinite flow of the universe, and from this place of trust it evolves into a knowing. Here, we get to live a life rich in experiences, which is the most expansive form of abundance.

One of the most profound transformations that occurs when embracing the concept of infinity is our relationship with death. The fear of death is, at its core, a fear of the unknown; a perceived endpoint that renders all our achievements and connections meaningless. However, when we understand that energy cannot be destroyed, only transformed, death loses its power to terrify. Death becomes a transition, a doorway to another form of existence. Instead of death being something we push away, we realize it's one of our greatest teachers; through death we're shown how to live. When we can surrender to the eternal Self, the fear of death transforms and instead we receive the gift of life. Appreciation for what's here, in this physical realm, in a physical body.

By embracing immortality while simultaneously embracing our impermanence, we liberate ourselves from the need to live small, safe, and confined lives. We begin to see our time on Earth as part of an eternal journey, one where each experience is an opportunity for growth and expression. This shift in perception allows us to live more boldly and authentically, knowing that every ending is simply the prelude to a new beginning.

When we welcome this concept of infinity, we liberate ourselves from the confines of linear thinking and step into a multidimensional way of being. Infinity brings freedom – freedom to create, to love, to evolve without limitation. It allows us to transcend the fear-based patterns that have kept us small and access the limitless potential of our true selves. From this place of infinite possibility, we can reimagine what it means to live an abundant life. We don't feel drawn to accumulating more things in order to feel abundant, as abundance comes from connecting to the wellspring of blessings that are already right here for us.

To step through the Infinity Gateway is to embrace the fullness of who we are – both human and divine, finite and infinite. It's to remember that we're not separate from the source of all creation, we're an expression of it. By dissolving the illusions of lack and limitation, we reclaim our rightful place as conscious creators in a universe that's endlessly expanding. The Violet Flame is there, lighting the way and encouraging us to move through it all.

Stepping Through the Infinity Gateway

As we've done in the previous chapters, prepare yourself a space so you can drop into this practice fully, ensuring you won't be disturbed. If possible, get outside in nature, where you can tangibly experience the vastness of creation: by the ocean, under the stars, in a forest, or on a hilltop with an open sky.

1. Remember to take a deep breath and gently ground yourself before you begin, so you feel anchored in your body and to the earth. Connect with the Violet Flame in a way that feels most nurturing for you (*or for more guidance, see page 16*).

2. Set the intention for this practice; that you're going to step through the Infinity Gateway and tune in to the abundance frequency, which is ever-present.

3. Close your eyes. Breathe deeply. With each inhale, soften into your body. With each exhale, let go of any tightness in your body, release the tension in your muscles, and surrender to being held by the earth. Feel the earth beneath you taking your full weight now so you can let go and completely soften, moving deeper and deeper into a relaxed state.

4. Start to see an Infinity Gateway appearing before you. As it becomes clearer you see that this gateway is a great portal of living light. It's vast yet intimate, golden and violet, shimmering with rainbow light prisms. It has no fixed form, it shifts, expands, pulses with the rhythm of creation. Stars spiral within it, galaxies turn, and through the center of this gateway is a deep void. This

is the threshold between the limited and the limitless. A passage into the eternal nature of existence.

5. As you step forward, the energy of the gateway wraps around you. As you move through it, begin now to feel the warmth of the Violet Flame filling you from within, this light moving through your physical vessel. Allow the Flame to light up any areas where you've previously felt restriction or lack, see these threads unraveling, dissolving into light. In moving through this gateway, you're no longer 'outside' abundance. You are within it. You are it.

6. Now, breathe. Inhale deeply. As the breath enters, feel it carrying golden light. Abundance fills your being, saturating every cell. Hold the breath. Let the energy settle. Feel it anchoring into your DNA, your consciousness, your reality. This is the frequency of expansion and receptivity.

7. Exhale slowly. Let the breath carry away the last traces of limitation. Surrender it all here slowly as you breathe outward. Hold the end of the exhale for a moment and feel the empty space this leaves within, the inner void, the place of infinite possibility. Repeat this cycle:

- Inhale: Abundance flows in.

- Hold: It anchors within you.

- Exhale: Surrender flows out.

- Hold: Connect with the void.

8. Feel the Violet Flame holding this light for you as it weaves through the experience, swirling around you and transforming

anything that attempts to come in to distract you, and bringing you back into presence. With each breath, you're programming the abundance into your being.

9. From this moment forward, every inhale reminds you of the infinite supply. Every exhale affirms your trust in the flow – there's nothing to hold onto as abundance is an infinite occurrence. Even after this practice ends, your breath will continue to anchor you in abundance. With every breath, you are expanding. With every breath, you are receiving. With every breath, you are abundant.

10. You soften your awareness and begin to expand it. You look to the stars; feel yourself stretching across galaxies, you're being interwoven with the great cosmic web. You are the stardust and the space between.

11. You now sense the Earth: the flowing rivers, the highest mountains, the forests breathing in rhythm with your own inhale and exhale. You're part of nature's intelligence, always connected.

12. You start to feel time dissolving. There's no past. No future. Only this moment exists. You're not confined to linear existence; you're an ever-expanding spiral. You're creation experiencing itself.

13. Now, shift your awareness and bring it right inward, to the universe within your body. Tune in to the beat of your heart; the same rhythmic pulse that moves us through expansion and contraction. Feel how it echoes through your entire being, steady and consistent, carrying the imprint of every moment you've ever lived.

14. Feel your breath moving through you; become aware of the way it enters, fills, and nourishes. The expansion of your chest, the

subtle cooling as air passes through your nostrils, this gentle rise and fall that's been with you since the moment you arrived into this life.

15. Bring awareness to your veins: your blood, pumping around you, an unbroken movement of energy flowing. Sense the aliveness in your fingertips, your toes, the spaces between your ribs. Notice how every part of you is in constant motion, even in stillness.

16. Turn your attention to the intelligence within you; the wisdom that beats your heart without instruction. The knowing that repairs your body, rejuvenates your cells, that whispers intuitions, that moves you in unseen ways. It speaks in sensation, in knowing, in subtle shifts of energy. Feel into this wisdom. Trust it. It's been guiding you since birth.

17. Expand your awareness beyond your body – journey deeper inward. Drop below the surface of muscle and bone, journey into your cells, and even deeper, into a single DNA molecule, into the void within this micro. Here, you're not just the physical. You're not just the human. You are formless, limitless, infinite. The body is the vessel, and you are the field of light moving through it.

You do not need to do anything.

You are already everything.

Linger in this space.

Breathe here for as long as you feel you need to.

18. As this practice comes to a close, take a final moment to feel this expansion within you out to the macro, as well as the retraction

into the micro. You're no longer separate from abundance. You are abundant. When you're ready, find a balanced resting place between the micro and macro, tuning in to your physical body and the space around it.

19. Begin to draw your awareness back to your surroundings. Feel the ground beneath you, the air around you, the pulse of life moving through you. And know this: The Infinity Gateway is always open. You can step through it at any moment, returning to the vastness, the truth, the remembrance.

+ ✦ +

Living Prayer

The Violet Flame reminds us that we're always in constant transformation, and as we walk this path, something miraculous happens: we stop searching for answers outside ourselves, and we realize we're the answer to our own prayer. There's a beauty in knowing that in every moment, no matter how lost or alone we may feel, we can call upon the Violet Flame. This presence is never separate from us; it moves through us, breathes through us, and responds to our call.

The Violet Flame lights us up so we can see that every thought infused with love is a prayer. Every moment of integrity is a prayer. Every act of kindness is a prayer. Every word said with compassion is a prayer.

As we deepen our relationship with the Violet Flame, a natural progression emerges where we move from self-centered desires to selfless service. In this space, the concept of prayer becomes more than spoken words and it transforms into a way of being. Through the alchemy of the Violet Flame we purify the layers of ego and meet ourselves fully – our light, our shadow, our longing, and our love. This authenticity births courage to live as a clear channel for universal love. From this space, service to others becomes a natural expression of who we are. Our prayers anchor us to grace, inviting us to see every circumstance as an opportunity to embody love. This is the transition from praying for ourselves or others, to becoming the prayer itself.

Becoming a living prayer is powerful. True service is the most natural thing in the world as it's simply an overflow of who we are. When we're aligned to abundance, our presence becomes a gift. The way we speak, create, move, listen, is all an act of service, to ourselves and others around us. Our service is the energy we bring to the world, what we put out, the impact we have.

What ripples does your presence create? This is your prayer, and this becomes your service.

Take a moment to reflect:

- In what ways am I already a living prayer?

- What energy do I bring into a space, even before I speak?

- How does my presence uplift, soothe, or inspire those around me?

- Where am I being called to bring more love, more kindness, more grace?

The answers to these questions are to be felt in the heart.

The Violet Flame lights us up with the awareness that we're always offering something (whether consciously or unconsciously) to the world and, in return, to ourselves. This offering is what we will magnetize back into our reality. However, within this, to give from the heart is to give without any expectation that we'll receive something in return.

Every word you speak carries a frequency. Words spoken from a place of love uplift. Words spoken from fear or judgment create discord and destruction. Not just to others, but also to ourselves. Before speaking, pause. Ask yourself: Is this an offering of love? If not, call in the Violet Flame to transform the message before it's spoken. Let your words become an extension of your prayer, let each footstep upon the Earth be made with grace. We don't need grand gestures to be of service. Every small act counts.

Small acts performed regularly become a living prayer. Here are some examples:

- Deep listening to another without interruption, so that they feel heard.

- Smiling at a stranger; it's contagious and mood-boosting.

- Paying someone a genuine compliment, uplifting them through your reflection.

- Making eye contact with someone (and you can also do this in the mirror to yourself), so they feel acknowledged and seen.

- Holding someone's hand when they need comfort, offering presence without words.

- Choosing sustainability, reducing your waste, and becoming a conscious consumer.

- Giving offerings to the earth, such as sowing seeds for trees, flowers, and herbs.

- Feeding the birds, butterflies and bees, and tending to wildlife, providing sustenance and care.

- Setting boundaries that honor your energy, saying 'no' with love when necessary.

- Placing your hand on your heart and taking a deep breath, giving a moment to return home to yourself.

- Blessing water before you drink it – water holds memory so infuse it with love.

To live as a prayer is to be in constant communion with the Divine and the environment surrounding us. It's to recognize that our very existence is an offering: learn, teach, inspire, share.

How we begin our day shapes the energy we carry forward. By anchoring ourselves in prayer each morning, we attune our hearts to the Divine and align with the flow of grace. It's important to note that true prayer doesn't have to be a set of rigid words, you can use prayer as an open doorway for you to connect to your heart, allowing yourself to flow from there. And remember, the most powerful prayer is the one you live.

This next practice is to support you in crafting your own personal prayer. You can build it into your daily routine to start each morning in the energy of prayer, setting the tone for the rest of the day.

Crafting a Daily Personal Prayer

1. Have your journal in front of you, and before beginning, take a few deep breaths to bring you into presence. Connect with the Violet Flame as you've done in previous practices (see page 16).

2. Take a moment to reflect on what you wish to bring forth in your life and into the world. Consider these prompts:

    + What energies do I wish to embody today?

    + How can I be of service through my presence?

    + How can I radiate more love?

3. Allow your heart to respond. Your prayer may be a few sentences or a full invocation. Flow with what wants to come through your heart. For example:

> 'Violet Flame, illuminate my day.
> Let my thoughts be pure, my words be kind,
> my actions be guided by love.
> May every step I take upon the Earth
> be gentle and intentional.
> I am a vessel of peace, a presence of compassion,
> a living prayer in motion.
> Violet Flame, move through me.
> Transform all I encounter into love.
> I walk as a living prayer today and always.
> For my highest good and the highest good of all.'

4. To complete your practice, visualize the Violet Flame radiating outward from your heart, blessing everything you'll encounter today – people, places, events.

5. Take a deep breath in, and as you exhale, say:

    'And so it is. I walk this day as a living prayer.'

6. When you're ready, open your eyes, carrying the energy of your prayer with you. If you feel called to do so, write your prayer down and place it on your altar for that day/week. Return to it daily or adapt it when the feeling arises.

This practice is more than just reciting words to speak your intention: through this you're stepping into that frequency. Each morning, as you align with the Violet Flame and the power of prayer, you strengthen your connection to the Divine. Remember, the most powerful prayer is the one you live. Let your presence be your prayer.

New Paradigm

Timelines are fluid, ever-shifting streams of potential. Each moment, each thought, each intention sends a ripple through the quantum field, opening doors to new outcomes, new futures. There are timelines where we keep ourselves in the cage of our own self-imposed limitations, where we choose the path of destruction. There are timelines where we liberate ourselves, feel the fear and do it anyway, where we choose the path of love. Every choice we make becomes a vote for the reality we're stepping into.

This is the dance of free will and fate. Both are alive within us. While the soul may arrive on Earth with a blueprint of lessons to learn and scenarios to experience for our soul growth, we're still the ones choosing how we arrive there. Do we repeat the loops or do we transform them?

A new paradigm is created when we align our choices, moment by moment, to the path of love. This is how we quantum leap onto a different timeline. When we hear the word quantum, many of us immediately think of sudden, dramatic shifts or giant leaps forward. In quantum physics however, a quantum change refers to the smallest possible unit of energy. An incredibly subtle, almost imperceptible movement. So, quantum leaps are actually about tiny, precise shifts that, when accumulated, result in profound change.

Through a series of small, aligned actions, shifts in thought, intention, and choice, when done consistently over time, the new paradigm emerges. These micro-adjustments, repeated and anchored, build the momentum that ultimately propels you into a new reality; much like a spiritual awakening, which can often feel sudden or revelatory. However, the ground beneath that awakening has usually been prepared over time. There's been a gradual softening, a slow unfolding, countless small moments of surrender and insight. Then one day, the shift in perception arrives and from that point, there's no turning back.

The Violet Flame shows us where we've been and where we can go, offering clarity when we make each decision. It helps us break free from inherited timelines, old conditioning, karmic threads. It brings light to unconscious loops and says: 'Here, now you get to choose again. What timeline would you like to experience?'

When we embody the universal love, speak with integrity, listen with compassion, and align our choices with the truth of who we are, we become the prayer. We become the transmission. So, the signal we send out becomes clearer, stronger, more magnetic. And when we infuse this way of being with the power of play, we open the door to an entirely new paradigm as the energy of play softens the grip of attachment. When we see life as a game, we begin to experiment, explore, and dance with possibility. It takes the seriousness out of it, and we stop clinging so tightly to *how* things must unfold, and we start allowing life to surprise us.

In the playground of manifestation, when we're less attached to specific outcomes, we're actually more aligned with the flow of the universe. We become cocreators who are willing to try, to adjust, to leap, and to laugh.

When we create a new paradigm, it's about remembering that the small steps are the most important, choosing love over fear, again and again. It's about recognizing that while we may live in a world of chaos, we're not helpless within it. We're cocreators. Thread-weavers. Bridge-builders. We become the peace, through anchoring to our hearts as home. The Violet Flame helps us access this with awareness, it becomes our mirror for expansion. It helps us pause before reacting, breathe before spiraling downward, and choose higher-vibrational timelines with intention.

It's the hand on our back as we quantum leap, and the warmth in our hearts when we speak our truth.

So here, I invite you to begin contemplating these questions:

- What does your soul truly long to experience?
- Which timeline feels aligned with your highest expression?
- What beliefs, habits, or energies still tether you to old paradigms and keep you looping?
- What small choices, made consistently, will begin to create a new timeline?
- And how would it feel to live as if the new timeline is already here?

With your answers to these questions, take time to envision and play with your imagination, as this holds the key to unlocking the Infinity Gateway. With every clear choice and, paradoxically, in every moment of surrender, you're walking yourself home through the Infinity Gateway and onto the timeline your soul has always known.

Becoming Your Future Self

1. As we've done in the previous practices, prepare yourself a space so you can drop into this practice fully, ensuring you won't be disturbed. Remember to take a deep breath and gently ground yourself before you begin, so you feel anchored in your body and to the earth. Connect with the Violet Flame in a way that feels most nurturing for you (or see page 16).

2. Set the intention for this practice: To meet your future Self and receive guidance from your highest timeline.

3. Close your eyes and take a deep breath in, feeling the gentle rise and fall of your chest. With each inhale, draw in violet light, and with each exhale, dissolve any tension.

4. Now picture yourself standing on a shimmering path of light. This is the path of your soul, glowing, infinite, stretching ahead into the realms of possibility. As you begin to walk forward, notice how the Violet Flame moves with you, lighting your way, gently lifting you toward your highest timeline. With each step, you feel yourself aligning more deeply with the truth of who you're becoming.

5. Up ahead, you begin to see a figure shining with radiant light. As you draw closer, you recognize the essence – it's you. This is your Future Self: the you who's already crossed thresholds, made quantum leaps, and fully embodied the life you dream of. Stand before them now. Notice how Future You is standing, what your presence emanates, how you smile, the energy you carry. Let yourself feel and fully receive yourself in this form. Gently ask:

    + What choices did you make to become who you are?

    + What wisdom do you have for me that will assist me in creating this timeline?

    + What do I need to remember?

6. Open your heart and listen. Maybe words arise, or perhaps you receive images, sensations, or a subtle knowing. Trust that whatever comes is perfect, and that your conscious mind will continue to unravel these gifts over time.

7. When you're ready, take a deep, steady breath. Imagine stepping forward and merging with your Future Self. Feel their light pouring into your body, their wisdom sinking into your bones, their love expanding your heart. You're not separate from them; you're weaving into their timeline now, aligning breath by breath.

8. Slowly, bring your awareness back to the room. Wiggle your fingers, your toes, take a grounding inhale, and softly open your eyes.

Before you rush ahead, take a few moments to journal any messages, emotions, or insights that surfaced.

CHAPTER 9

Returning to One

'You are a ripple of the whole,'
the Violet Flame whispered through its warm glow.
'You have moved through the labyrinth of separation,
and now comes a return to the One.'

I closed my eyes, feeling the Flame's light, its essence
touching the deepest corners of my soul.
'How do I return' I asked, 'when the
world feels so divided, when I sometimes
still feel fractured within myself?'

The Violet Flame flickered gently, a soothing softness
within its glow. 'You do not need to seek out the One,'
it said. 'You are already within it. You return,
with the remembering: that separation is the
grand illusion, a veil woven by the mind,
to urge you to explore the depths of experience.
Yet the heart knows the truth:
Every moment, every being, every shadow,
and every light is an echo of the whole.
And as each individual begins to confront their own
shadows with acceptance and an open heart,
the collective shadows lift, returning
the whole back to light.'

Its words stirred something within me as I paused
for a moment. 'Why must I feel so separate, so alone?'
I asked. 'Why do I ache to return to something I have
never truly left?' I felt the discomfort of separation,
as if I had just been severed from the womb.

*The violet hues pulsed brighter, the fire revealing
endless spirals of which the depth fascinated me.
'Because it's from the forgetting, you have learned.
Even "alone" broken down is "all one." Through the illusion
of separation, you have come to know the beauty of unity.
Every encounter, every lesson, has been guiding you back.
Each shadow you've embraced, each light you've tended to,
has brought the collective closer to the truth.
For as you heal yourself, you heal the whole.'*

*I felt the paradox of both longing and fulfillment.
'What does it mean to truly return?' I asked.
'What does it look like to live in Oneness?'*

*The Violet Flame danced with its radiant intensity,
its light weaving geometric fractals –
too intricate for the eye to comprehend.
'To return to the One is to be fully in this life,
embodied, and with presence.
So you can see the Divine in all things.
To look into the eyes of another and recognize yourself.
To walk through life with an open heart,
knowing that every experience, joyful or painful,
is a reflection of all that is sacred.
It is to dissolve the illusion of "mine" and "yours,"
and to live in the knowing that all is "ours."'*

*The Flame became almost still for a moment,
its light turning inward, drawing me with it.
'In this Oneness, there is no lack,' it continued,
'No judgment, no separation. There is only love,
infinite and all-encompassing. And as you embody this
truth, you carry the frequency of union into the world,
and through you, the New Earth is born.'*

*Tears streamed down my face as its words reached a
place never touched before. 'And what of the shadows?'
I whispered. 'The ones we still carry as a collective?'*

*The Flame's light softened, 'Do not fear these shadows,'
it said. 'As each of your shadows are cleared through love,
the collective light grows brighter. As you meet yourself
with acceptance, you also meet others from this place.
This is how the whole is restored – no longer
rejecting, avoiding, shaming, and blaming.
As you continue to integrate and bring love to
your own shadows, you end the war within.
This illuminates the path for others to do the same.
Through the micro-macro reflection.
This is how we return together, as One.'*

*I felt the Violet Flame glowing within me,
becoming the hearth of my bodily home.
'What lies beyond the return?' I asked softly.*

*The Flame's voice now sounded like a gentle hum.
'Beyond the return is the beginning. As you merge
back into the One, you will find yourself everywhere.
In everyone and everything. And from this place of
wholeness, you will cocreate the New Earth;
a world rooted in love, unity, peace, and beauty.
You will carry the Violet Flame within you,
a torch lighting the way for all beings.
For you are the Divine Beloved's living expression.'*

*And as the Violet Flame's light settled into my heart,
I knew in that moment: Heaven is right here,
in this breath, in this body, in this life. I don't
need to seek it elsewhere, as there is nowhere else to go.
Yet the imagination of creation will forever move me.
And in this continuous spiral of creation,
I AM eternal as One.*

'Oneness' – how does one capture the experience of it in words? In a moment, time stops, your heart blasts you open to a pure state of awe for the ways in which creation moves through you. It feels like every atom of existence is pulsing through the entirety of your being. You can see every star in the sky, every planet in rotation, and every grain of sand on the land. You feel every footstep that's ever been walked, every breath that's ever been taken. You can hear every heart that's ever beaten, and every word that's ever been sung. You feel every single drop of rain that's ever fallen, and the expanse of the ocean within each drop. You can see how every event, experience, and moment in time is all woven together through threads and fractals.

Oneness is to experience both ecstatic bliss and excruciating pain: the paradoxical rhythm of the universe itself. You feel the pulse of creation, the expansion and contraction, until all distinctions dissolve. In the stillness, all that remains is the void. Completely still, you move through the nothingness that is, paradoxically, everything. Surrounded by sound while suspended in an infinite silence, it becomes clear that even 'nothing' cannot cease to exist.

Creation is perpetual. There is no beginning, no end, only the continuous unfolding of life. The Violet Flame burns eternally here, ensuring change is continuous. No moment can ever be repeated, and yet everything is always echoing itself in new forms. Creation humbles us. It's a living algorithm, constantly mirroring back our energy, offering loops, patterns, paradoxes, and reflections. Just when we think we've deciphered its mysteries, it shifts, presenting something new to explore.

Courageous soul, thank you for being here and making it this far. These pages I've shared with you are my lived experience, and now they are yours, too! Through writing this book, I've re-experienced the Violet Flame in new ways. It's felt multidimensional – at times I'd look up from the screen only to see the very words I'd just written manifesting into physical reality right in front of my eyes. It's been pure magic. Such is the power of the Violet Flame, weaving seen and unseen worlds together, forever illuminating shadows, bridging divides, creating unions, inviting us forward to live our highest purpose.

Well done, you've reached the last chapter of this book. And yet, as eternity suggests, there really is no end. So let this not be an ending, but the beginning of something infinite. For you are not separate from the One, you are the One, returning to itself.

This last chapter is not the end of the book, it's actually an invitation, to begin again. I encourage you to return to Chapter 1 of this book, with new eyes and an open heart, carrying all that you've integrated from this journey with the Violet Flame. Each page will meet you differently every time, offering you deeper layers – an ever-expanding spiral.

I celebrate your bravery in walking this path – to embrace your shadows and ignite your higher purpose is no small thing. You're part of this unfolding story – now, too, you're the pages of this book, you're the violet light of transformation, and you're living in a world that deeply needs your expression. May the Violet Flame continue to be a frequency to live by, as you're now the living Flame. You're the torchbearer of the New Earth. And wherever you walk, you illuminate the way.

Birthing the New Earth with the Violet Flame of Unity

1. Before you start, ground yourself and connect with the Violet Flame in your own way so you're anchored and ready for this meditation (or see page 16).

2. Close your eyes and take a deep breath in, feeling the gentle rise and fall of your chest. With each inhale, draw in violet light, and with each exhale, release any tension. Notice if there's any lingering sense of separation, as you begin to feel heavier and more relaxed with each breath, feeling yourself soften and surrender, allowing the ground to hold you as you feel your aura expanding outward.

3. Now call the Violet Flame into your awareness – see, sense, and feel the violet light beginning to flicker, alive with intelligence, the fire dancing and welcoming you home to the present moment. Step forward and feel this sacred fire ignite within your heart, its warmth expanding outward, dissolving the illusion of separation. Feel it moving through your entire being, illuminating every cell with the remembrance of Oneness.

4. Now see this Violet Flame expanding, rippling out across the Earth, touching every continent, every ocean, every living being. Watch as the planet begins to glow with this sacred fire of transformation. The air becomes crystalline clear, charged with life force. The sunlight spills like golden nectar, warm and bright. Every tree stands tall, its leaves shimmering green, pulsing with energy and wisdom. Flowers bloom in vibrant, rainbow colors, releasing fragrances that soothe the soul. The rivers and oceans are pure, their waters glistening like liquid light, filled with life, thriving, abundant.

5. Now turn your awareness to the people. Their faces are illuminated, their eyes bright with recognition. Seeing each other not as strangers, but as reflections of the same divine source. Borders fade. Judgment dissolves. Hearts open. Compassion flows freely. See them moving with grace and presence, fully embodied in their divinity. There's no rush, no fear, no striving; only flow, harmony, and deep peace. Children laugh as they play freely in nature, their spirits untamed, their joy infectious. Communities gather in love, sharing, cocreating, honoring one another.

6. Feel into this New Earth. Abundance flows effortlessly — health, vitality, love, joy, creativity. Every soul is thriving. Every being is in perfect harmony with their own energy, their own divine essence. The wisdom of the body is awakened, and healing is natural, instantaneous rejuvenation. Every hand that touches the earth does so with reverence, and in return, the earth provides in overflowing bounty — food that nourishes not just the body but the soul; water that's alive and sparkles like liquid gold; air that feels like vitality filling your lungs with pure life force.

7. Breathe it in. Feel the pulse of creation itself moving through you. This is not a dream. This is a memory from the future, a world that already exists in the field of possibility.

8. See yourself here, standing in this world: whole, radiant, peaceful. You're not separate from this vision – you are this vision. And as you hold this frequency of unity, love, and abundance, you become an anchor for it; it's here now, birthed through the consciousness you're anchoring in this very moment.

9. Take a deep breath in, feeling the Violet Flame still bright within you, a force of transformation. With every thought of love, every act of kindness, every breath taken in awareness, you are the rising. As you exhale, know that you're already a part of this reality – and that through your very being, the New Earth is being born.

10. When you're ready, gently return to the present moment, carrying this frequency of unity with you. The Great Awakening has already begun – and you are a light within it.

Final Thoughts

The journey with the Violet Flame begins as a deeply personal alchemy. It transforms us through illuminating our shadows so they can be accepted and integrated, restoring our connection to universal love. For those who've walked this path, who've allowed the Flame to cleanse and transmute their own inner world, who understand the micro-macro mirror, and have gained a sense of Oneness, a natural question arises: How can I offer the Violet Flame to the world? The answer is: You direct the Violet Flame.

Throughout the pages of this book, you'll have gained the awareness that by invoking the Violet Flame within, you've triggered a whole personal healing journey. And through the law of Oneness, this has a ripple effect on the collective healing. To use the Flame in an intentional way to bring service to the world is such a beautiful act of universal love.

As the Violet Flame is a force of love that spans beyond time and space, it flows through all who are willing to receive it with an open heart. It travels through the infinite timelines. And through this journey, we become a living prayer and an instrument of grace, using the Flame to uplift and support humanity. In raising our own vibration, we naturally shape the world around us, radiating the energy of transformation for ourselves and all beings.

Understanding the Infinity Gateway (*see page 164*) allows us to see that the Violet Flame operates beyond the constraints of linear time. In this physical reality, we appear to experience events in a sequence: past, present, future. However, the energetic imprint of all these experiences remains woven into the collective field. Just as we hold memories, emotions, and karma within our own energy bodies, so too, the Earth carries the imprints of history, the present moment, and future happenings within its ley lines, at sacred sites, and through the collective consciousness. To work with the Violet Flame for world healing is to recognize that everything is energy. Every event, every emotion, every moment of struggle or joy, carries a vibration. The Violet Flame offers us a way to shift, refine, transform, and elevate these frequencies.

So, when we invoke the Violet Flame for world healing, we're not bound by time. We can direct its energy toward past events, to be a light of hope amid the density of war, injustice, and suffering. We can send it to the present moment, holding space for transformation in times of crisis. We can offer it to the future, laying the foundations for a more harmonious reality. In this way, working with the Violet Flame becomes an act of service to the entire web of existence. We become Keepers of the Flame, weaving it through the timelines of humanity itself.

Across the world there's been war, division, environmental destruction, and injustice – which all weigh heavily upon the collective heart. Just as the Violet Flame teaches us to meet our own shadows with love, so too, can we extend this wisdom to the world. We don't need to carry the weight of global suffering, nor do we need to be consumed by despair. Instead, we can take empowered action through prayer, intention, and energy work. By invoking the Violet Flame, we hold a space where transformation can occur through love.

When we hear of a tragic event, when we feel overwhelmed by worldly affairs, it can cause us to close our hearts, feel disempowered, or fall into a state of hopelessness. This creates a denser vibration, and we match these events energetically. The outcome of this is that we magnetize and manifest more of it, which keeps us experiencing more of the same within our reality.

Instead, pause. Take a breath. Call upon the Violet Flame. Envision it enveloping the situation, surrounding all involved, dissolving the heaviness, and restoring harmony. We must not deny the current reality or bypass it; however, we can choose to respond differently so we can be active participants in its healing. Every time you do this, you become a point of light in the collective. Your presence, your prayer, has more impact than you may ever fully realize. It only takes one candle to light up a room.

And just as individuals accumulate karma through their choices and actions, so too does humanity as a whole. Wars, exploitation, and cycles of suffering leave energetic imprints that continue to ripple through the generations. These imprints shape reality, influencing patterns of fear, separation, and disharmony. The Violet Flame is one of the most powerful tools for clearing collective karma. By invoking it with intention, we participate in the dissolution of old wounds and outdated structures. We're not powerless against historical events; we're actively contributing to its rewriting through changing the future.

To call on and connect with the Violet Flame for collective karma, one must approach with a pure heart. That means bringing compassion rather than blame or judgment, which can be challenging. However, by invoking the Forgiveness Flame, we can offer love where there's been pain. It's about standing in the knowing that all beings, no matter their actions, are part of the great unfolding, and a part of the whole.

World Healing

This can be carried out at your Violet Flame altar if you've created one (it acts as an anchor and container as it's already infused with the intention of transformation and alchemy). However, if you feel a calling to go out into nature, seek a place where the Earth's energy is strong: a site along one of the planet's ley lines, a sacred well, an ancient standing stone, or even a quiet place that simply feels alive beneath your feet. These natural energy points act as amplifiers, allowing the vibration you send to be carried through the Earth's energetic grid, rippling outward across the globe.

Preparing for World Healing

1. Remember to take a deep breath and gently ground yourself before you begin, so you feel anchored in your body and to the earth.

2. Light a candle and connect with the Violet Flame in a way that feels most nurturing for you (see page 16).

3. Set the intention for this practice: to send the Violet Flame out for collective healing.

4. Close your eyes and begin to see the Violet Flame within you, pulsing at the center of your being, radiant and alive. As you breathe, allow it to expand, moving through your energy field, flowing through your heart.

5. Call upon the Keepers of the Violet Flame – Mary Magdalene, Yeshua, Saint Germain, Lady Portia, Holy Amethyst, and Archangel Zadkiel – inviting them to stand beside you to assist with this practice.

Sending the Violet Flame to World Events

1. Recall a situation in the world that's in need of healing. It may be a crisis unfolding in the present, a conflict, an environmental issue, or perhaps it's something you've been witnessing in the collective – a dense or heavy energy lingering in the field.

2. Don't attach to the pain or the fear surrounding it. Instead, see the Violet Flame enveloping the entire situation, swirling around it like a living force, dissolving discord, transforming shadow into light, bringing a silent holding to everyone involved. Keep the vision of this event wrapped in the Flame's embrace. Whisper these words, or allow your heart to speak its own prayer:

> 'Violet Flame of Transformation, move through this place, through this moment in time. Dissolve all that is not love.

> *Restore balance where there is chaos. Peace where there is pain. Harmony where there is discord. Love where there is fear. For the highest good of all, so it is.'*

3. Hold this vision a moment longer, then release it. Trust that the energy has been received.

Sending Distance Healing to Individuals or Groups

1. If there are specific souls in need of support, whether they're known to you or not, hold them gently in your awareness now. If you have a list of names, you may speak them aloud or simply bring them into your heart.

2. See the Violet Flame flowing from your palms, your heart, your entire being, surrounding each person in its gentle violet light. There's no need to 'fix' or change anything, only to offer them this light, this grace, this warmth, this holding, this possibility of receiving love.

3. You may call upon the Keepers of the Flame to assist you:

> *'Mary Magdalene, Yeshua, Saint Germain, Lady Portia, Holy Amethyst, and Archangel Zadkiel, walk beside these souls. May they receive the love that is their birthright. May their suffering be lifted, their hearts restored, their path illuminated. May they remember who they truly are. For their highest good and the highest good of all. So it is.'*

4. Breathe deeply, knowing that the energy has been sent, and that it will find its way to them in perfect timing.

Healing Historical Timelines with the Violet Flame

1. If a particular moment in history calls to you, trust it. Perhaps it's an era of great division, an ancestral wound, or a time of suffering that still lingers in the collective consciousness. Hold this moment within your awareness, not as something that's distant but as something that still echoes within the energy of the present.

2. See the Violet Flame burning through time, pouring into the 'past,' dissolving the weight of sorrow, lifting the pain, offering release. See the timelines shifting as you send the energy of the Violet Flame. Watch as the Flame moves through the hearts of those who lived through this moment, offering them peace, freedom, and the remembrance of their divinity.

3. With deep reverence, speak these words:

   'Through the eternal light of the Violet Flame, I send healing across all time and space. May all who have suffered find peace. May the echoes of pain dissolve, leaving only love as the pathway forward. For the highest good of all. So it is.'

4. Take a breath and allow the vision to settle.

Closing the Practice

1. As this practice comes to completion, return to your own heart. See the Violet Flame resting there, alive within you, a constant presence of transformation. You are not separate from this energy – you are the Violet Flame embodied.

2. Offer a final prayer of gratitude to the Keepers of the Flame, to the Earth, to the divine intelligence that's woven this moment into being.

3. If you're at your altar, you may extinguish your candle now, knowing that its light continues to burn in the unseen. If you're in nature, offer a moment of silence to the earth beneath you, allowing your energy to root, steady and strong.

When we dedicate ourselves to this work, we step into our true power. We are no longer passive observers of the world's suffering, instead, we are active participants in its becoming. The Violet Flame moves through us; we transform through our choices. Every time we choose love over fear, forgiveness over resentment, compassion over judgment, and rejuvenation over destruction, we become a living embodiment of the Flame.

What if I told you that the secret is no longer hidden.
And this sacred fire has become far more than a
concept you've read about in the pages of this book.
You are it now: a living transmission of the Violet Flame.
You have walked with the Flame to burn
through the shadows, softened in surrender,
forgiven what was forgotten, and remembered.
As the veil has lifted, you have transcended the confines
of individual experience and connected to universal love.
You have become your prayer,
and together with the Violet Flame,
you are the alchemy.

This is the path of the alchemist,
the healer, the world-changer.
This is the path of those who dare to
dream of a world reborn in love.
And it is through our daily choices,
our unwavering devotion, and
carrying the Violet Flame within,
that this dream becomes lived reality.

With deepest gratitude, I thank you:
for your courage to invoke the Violet Flame,
for opening up to blazing transformation,
for integrating all parts, for remembering
your essence, for being universal love,
for being the piece to create peace.
And with this, birthing the New Earth.

I'll meet you forward,
back at Chapter One…

Love, Violet xx

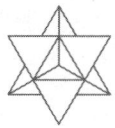

Acknowledgments

The Violet Flame – I thank you for lighting me up and being the force that continuously awakens, transforms, and expands me in the most magical ways.

The strong women in my family: my mum, Deborah; my sister, Robin; and my aunty, Della. You have shown me the deepest unconditional love throughout my life. Thank you for always celebrating me, wholeheartedly accepting me (even with all my weird and wonderful ways), and for being there for me through the highs and lows.

Thank you to the father figures in my life: my dad, John, and my stepdad, Gordon. You have both contributed to my growth in different ways. I appreciate the men that you are.

My magical soul sister, Karen – thank you for seeing me, believing in me, and for being my fairy godmother, forever reminding me of what's possible when I most need to see it. I am extremely grateful for your presence in my life.

Thank you to the beautiful divine feminine reflections I have had with special sisters in my life: Amanda, Emma, and Nicole. You have inspired me and, through your presence, you've gifted me breadcrumbs of wisdom along this journey. And to Annabelle, whom I met at the Writers' Workshop – thank you for being a sounding board when I needed it most and for being one of my cheerleaders.

Special soul Sage – you have been my masculine anchor throughout this journey. You've been by my side, encouraging me and supporting me by holding space, and providing for me in ways I didn't even know I needed. Through your mirror, I'm reminded every day of what I'm capable of. Thank you for your magic.

To the whole Hay House team – what an absolute gift it has been to collaborate with you. Thank you for recognizing the importance of sharing the Violet Flame with the world. To Michelle – I'll never forget the moment when you called to tell me I'd won the Writers' Workshop. To Kezia – thank you for matching my excitement from the very beginning, especially in those first few months as I processed the reality of becoming a published Hay House author. To Rebecca – thank you for bringing all the pieces together and keeping everything on track. And a special thank you to Cathy, who I worked so closely with while writing and editing. We shared such a beautiful connection. Thank you for all the support, encouragement, and reassurance – and for your editing wizardry.

Lastly, thank you to all the beloved souls I've met along this journey – each of you has touched my heart. To the faery community, sister circles, and Temple of the Feminine Flame – you know who you are.

Violet Skies

About the Author

Violet Skies is an intuitive, healer, and guide whose connection with the Violet Flame is both intimate and profound. This sacred relationship was first sparked by a near-death experience and deepened through a powerful spiritual awakening following the loss of a close family member.

At the heart of Violet's work is The Temple of the Feminine Flame – a sanctuary she cofounded to empower women to step into more liberated versions of themselves, embrace their cyclic nature, and cultivate a strong community rooted in sisterhood.

With an extensive background in a range of healing modalities, Violet brings insight and depth to her work. She offers Magdalene Rose Oracle Readings and Healing sessions that support one-on-one soul exploration, providing space for deep realizations and a greater sense of clarity and awareness.

Violet has been facilitating women's circles, seasonal ceremonies, workshops, and retreats – both in-person and online – since 2019.

@iam.violetskies
@templeofthefeminineflame
www.violetskieshealing.com

We hope you enjoyed this Hay House book. If you'd like to receive our online catalogue featuring additional information on Hay House books and products, please contact:

Hay House UK Ltd
1st Floor, Crawford Corner,
91–93 Baker Street, London W1U 6QQ
Tel: +44 (0)20 3927 7290; www.hayhouse.co.uk

Published in the United States of America by:
Hay House LLC
PO Box 5100, Carlsbad, CA 92018-5100
Tel: (760) 431-7695 or (800) 654-5126
www.hayhouse.com

Published in Australia by:
Hay House Australia Publishing Pty Ltd
18/36 Ralph St., Alexandria NSW 2015
Tel: +61 (02) 9669 4299
www.hayhouse.com.au

Published in India by:
Hay House Publishers (India) Pvt Ltd
Muskaan Complex, Plot No. 3,
B-2, Vasant Kunj, New Delhi 110 070
Tel: +91 11 41761620
www.hayhouse.co.in

Let Your Soul Grow

Experience life-changing transformation – one video at a time – with guidance from the world's leading experts.

www.healyourlifeplus.com

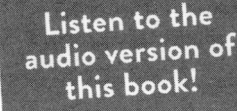

CONNECT WITH
HAY HOUSE
ONLINE

🌐 hayhouse.co.uk   **f** @hayhouse

📷 @hayhouseuk   🦋 @hayhouseuk.bsky.social

♪ @hayhouseuk   ▶ @HayHousePresents

Find out all about our latest books & card decks • Be the first to know about exclusive discounts • Interact with our authors in live broadcasts • Celebrate the cycle of the seasons with us • Watch free videos from your favourite authors • Connect with like-minded souls

'*The gateways to wisdom and knowledge are always open.*'

Louise Hay